SEVENTEEN
MISSIONS TO SAVE
THE WORLD

SEVENTEEN
MISSIONS TO SAVE
THE WORLD

LEYTH SHARAF

ISBN: 978-1-78324-370-9

This book is a work of fiction. Any resemblance
to actual persons, living or dead, events or
locales is entirely coincidental.

DISCLAIMER

This is a work of fiction. Any names, characters, businesses, organizations, places, events, or incidents are either the product of the author's imagination or are used in a fictitious manner. Any resemblance to actual persons, living or dead, or actual events is purely coincidental.

References to historical figures, locations, or real-world issues are included for narrative purposes and do not imply endorsement, criticism, or affiliation with any real individuals, corporations, or institutions. The author does not intend to slander, defame, or harm the reputation of any entity, person, or group.

This book is dedicated to

His Royal Highness Crown Prince Al Hussein bin Abdullah II,
whose vision for innovation, sustainability, and youth empowerment
continues to inspire a new generation of changemakers.
May this book contribute, in some small way, to the brighter
future His Royal Highness envisions for Jordan and the world.

CONTENTS

INTRODUCTION

The Basketball Game That Opened Time

Look, I didn't plan on saving the world. I was just trying to win a basketball game.

But apparently, fate had decided that I, Leyth Sharaf, a completely normal (okay, semi-normal) high school student at Dubai College, would become the one responsible for saving the entire planet. No pressure, right?

It all started on a Friday afternoon, towards the end of the championship game. We were playing the Abu Dhabi Falcons, and the gym felt like it was about to explode from all the excitement. The bleachers on both sides were packed, with fans yelling, each side trying to out-shout the other. But it was our home court, so our side was fuller, louder, buzzing with that kind of energy you only get when your whole school's counting on you.

My hands were slick on the ball. I bounced it twice—thump, thump—feeling the rubber thump back against my palm. It was a tie game. Ten seconds left. My heart pounded loud enough to drown out the crowd.

And that's when it happened, the moment the world cracked open.

Literally.

The lights flickered. A blast of wind tore through the gym like a rogue tornado, flinging water bottles, phones and a very startled crowd in every direction. The ground rumbled aggressively, like something ancient was waking up below the gym. People started screaming. Someone yelled, "earthquake!" but this wasn't the kind you could measure on the Richter scale.

The scoreboard sparked and exploded in a shower of blue light. Our coach dove behind the bench. Students ran for the exits, tripping over gym bags and dropping popcorn.

Then it appeared. Right at center court, a portal, shimmering, rippling like liquid glass, hovered a foot off the floor. And stepping out of it was the most extraordinary person I had ever seen.

She was tall—like *could dunk a basketball without jumping* tall. Her bronze skin glowed, flawless and smooth, like it had been sculpted from stardust. Her wild black curls had a mind of their own, twisting and shifting around her head like Medusa's serpents.

Her deep blue cape streaked with flickering constellations, floated dramatically behind her.

And just when I thought things couldn't get weirder, I noticed the rest of her outfit. She was wearing a basketball uniform. Her silver jersey and matching shorts glimmered like starlight woven into mesh, with silver high-tops, laced tight like she was prepared to win an intergalactic basketball competition.

She was Harlem Globetrotters meets Nike. She spun a glowing basketball on her fingertip, not just spinning ... orbiting ... like the laws of physics had given up trying to contain her. Then, with a flick of her wrist, she launched it behind her back, caught it midair, rolled it down her arm, and dribbled between her legs so fast I barely saw it happen.

"I am The Reminder," she said. "I show people what happens when they forget."

I blinked. "Forget what? Homework?" I asked. "Because I'm

pretty sure I forgot to do my English essay, and Mr. Simpson is going to—"

"Forget their responsibilities to the world," she cut me off. Which was rude, but okay.

"The future is collapsing," she continued, as if this was totally normal news. "And only you can fix it."

She gestured, and the ball floating beside her turned into a globe. Images swirled around it: floods, fires, poverty, unemployment.

"Seventeen disasters," she said. "Seventeen ways everything goes completely, irreversibly wrong."

I took a step back, clutching my basketball like a life jacket.

Behind me, someone muttered, "cool, I've officially lost it."

That was Ellie, she played power forward on our team. She was gripping my sleeve like I was about to be abducted by aliens.

"You see this, right?" she whispered.

"Yep," I said. "Definitely."

I should've told the glowing amazon to hold that thought until after the game.

Instead, I stood there like a stunned goldfish.

"What do you mean?" I croaked.

The Reminder sighed, like this whole "explaining world doom" gig was getting old.

"The world is spiraling toward catastrophe," she repeated sternly. "Famine, poverty, climate collapse, war. You must go back in time and prevent seventeen crises before it's too late."

Ellie made a sound somewhere between a gasp and a wheeze. "Time travel? Oh, no. Nope. Nope. Nope. Not happening."

"Seventeen doomed futures await you," The Reminder went on, ignoring Ellie's full meltdown. "Each one shows a world devastated by a different crisis. You must return and change the present before each disaster becomes inevitable."

I opened my mouth to argue. I had arguments! Logical ones! Like: I have a physics exam next week! Or, I'm only fifteen!

But at that moment, Ellie did something very Ellie.

She grabbed my arm.

Now, in her defense, she was trying to yank me back, away from the cosmic basketball player and the swirling time vortex.

But she yanked too hard.

And we both stumbled forward.

The portal surged outward, sucking us in like we were loose socks in the world's most powerful washing machine.

"OMG!" Ellie yelled.

And then we were falling.

Spinning.

Weightless.

My stomach was somewhere near my ears.

The gym was gone.

Dubai disappeared.

Even gravity seemed to be taking a break. Maybe I should have paid more attention in science class because I don't remember reading about all this in the textbook.

And just like that, we were flung straight into Mission Number One.

ONE

–2050–

THE PRICE OF POVERTY

SDG 1: No Poverty

I landed with a *thwack* so loud it probably registered on the moon. Not just any fall—oh no. This was a whopper. It was a 50-out-of-10, spine-tingling, tooth-rattling, absolutely outrageous kind of fall. My elbows went east, my knees went west, and my sanity vanished entirely.

Ellie landed next to me with an even louder *oof*, rolling to a stop against something that smelled like garbage. "Okay," she groaned, "time portals need to come with seatbelts and air fresheners!"

We sat up slowly.

And froze.

We were in Rome. But this wasn't *any* version of Rome I'd seen before.

Rome's ancient grandeur was gone. Its once-bustling piazzas and ornate facades now stood in eerie silence. Skyscrapers, new and old, jutted into the sky like broken teeth, their windows shattered, their frames half-eaten by rust. The Colosseum loomed like a ghost, its proud arches charred and crumbling. St. Peter's Basilica? A cracked ruin.

The street ahead was a canyon of desperation. Shanties built from rusted metal, plastic covers and scraps of wood lined the sidewalks. People lay curled in alleyways under piles of clothes and newspapers. Mothers rocked infants wrapped in old curtains. Skeletal children swarmed the intersections and banged on car windows, holding out their boney hands, hoping for spare change.

We walked under an overpass where entire families were sleeping on flattened cardboard. A teenager dug through a toppled dumpster, tugging at a banana peel like it was treasure. Nearby, an old woman tried to warm her hands over a burning tire, her palms shaking.

Ellie's voice cracked. "Leyth... this is poverty like I have never seen before."

I couldn't speak. My throat felt too tight.

A raspy voice spoke behind us. "This is the first future I wanted you to witness, so you can see what's in store if you don't go back in time and change things."

We spun around.

A person stood there. No ... a shifting *something*. Their form flickered, morphing between ages, genders, and even clothes. One second, they were a desperate father begging for food to feed his family, next, a small child in rags. Its voice wavered, like it was coming from different mouths at once.

I swallowed hard. "Who—what—are you?"

The shapes suddenly merged into a single figure, the same figure we saw back at the very start. The Reminder.

Her voice was quieter now. "Remember what I told you. Seventeen futures. Seventeen chances to go back and fix them."

A chill crawled down my spine. "But how?"

The Reminder's form flickered again, settling into the shape of a young woman with sunken eyes. "You have to convince humans that Earth's equilibrium needs to be rebalanced. You can start by redistributing resources."

I looked around, at the desperation around us. *Could this really be our future?*

The Reminder tilted her head. "You still have a chance to turn things around, but you don't have very long."

The air around us shimmered. A powerful force yanked us backward. The world twisted and spun—

And we landed in the middle of a crowded street in Rome. The year: 2025.

TWO

– 2 0 2 5 –

FROM POVERTY TO PROSPERITY

SDG 1: No Poverty

Ellie sat beside me, brushing gravel off her knees. "Why are we falling again? Can't we time travel with a parachute or something?"

I didn't have time to answer. A Vespa swerved past, missing me by inches.

"Guarda dove vai!" ("Watch where you're going!") the driver barked, speeding off toward Piazza Venezia.

I stumbled back, grabbing Ellie's arm.

At first glance, Rome looked normal. The streets bustled like any other day; suits clicking past on polished shoes, tourists posing on corners, mopeds weaving through traffic like they owned the place. But there were signs of poverty if you paid attention. A mother and father huddled on a street corner near Piazza Venezia, their three kids curled against them under a tattered blanket with a cardboard sign beside them reading *Abbiamo fame—We are hungry.* Two barefoot children wandered between stopped cars at an intersection, holding out plastic cups while drivers pretended not to see. Near the back of a gelato shop, a teenager rummaged through a dumpster, pulling out a bruised banana and a crushed water bottle like it was treasure. Every alley seemed to hold someone—an old man sleeping under a bridge made of flattened boxes, a woman boiling water over a makeshift fire, her belongings stacked in shopping bags beside her.

We walked further down the road and found two rusted bikes leaning against a chain-link fence and, without even discussing it, hopped on. Our wheels rattled down narrow cobbled streets. That's when we noticed something else.

The buildings.

So many were empty. Dusty windows. Boards over the doors.

That's when the idea hit.

I slowed to a stop in front of a crumbling old apartment building with vines growing out of the mailbox. "Wait a second," why are all these people on the streets... when there are empty buildings everywhere?"

Ellie pulled up beside me, "you're right. That doesn't make any sense."

I turned toward her.

"What if we turned abandoned buildings into shared homes, and gave people the chance to rebuild them from the inside out?

Ellie grinned. "Now *that's* an idea worth time-traveling for."

The Pitch

Later that week, we made our way to the municipal headquarters and requested a meeting with Rome's Deputy Mayor for Urban

Development.

The receptionist eyed us like we were tourists who'd wandered in by mistake. I couldn't blame her.

She looked up. "Ha un appuntamento?"—"do you have an appointment?"

I spoke in English, but most of Rome's business people understood it.

"No," I said, "but if he's running for another term, he'll want to hear our proposal."

Ellie whispered, "Oh great, we're getting arrested in record time."

Ten minutes later, we were sitting across from the mayor while sipping expressos.

We presented our proposal: take abandoned, city-owned buildings and turn them into shared housing for low-income families. The ground floor of each building? Transform them into co-op businesses owned and operated by the residents—bakeries, tailoring shops, repair centers, and more.

The Deputy Mayor leaned back in his chair. "E come possiamo sapere che funzionerà davvero?"—"And how can we know it will actually work?"

Ellie didn't miss a beat. "Because what you're doing now isn't."

He raised an eyebrow.

I leaned in. "Look outside. The food pantry lines. The kids begging at intersections. People sleeping under ancient monuments while tourists take selfies."

There was a pause. A long one.

Then, to our shock, he chuckled. "You two," he said, "remind me of my sister's kids. Full of chaos. And somehow... sometimes, they're right."

He tapped his pen twice on the desk.

"Va bene. Let's try it in one district. Now get out before I change my mind."

We didn't need to be told twice. We were out the door in record time, practically skipping down the marble steps.

The Ripple Effect

Approval came quickly. The first building—cracked walls, dusty stairwells, long forgotten by the city, was suddenly alive again.

Within weeks, the first building was buzzing with activity; residents helping each other install flooring, repaint walls, and hang new doors.

Downstairs, businesses came alive too. A community-run bakery opened up. A tailor in the building set up a corner shop, training others on how to hem, patch, and stitch. An unemployed chef opened up a community-run restaurant and trained residents for different positions. Each business was run by a team of residents, who, just weeks earlier, had stood in food lines.

Each shop became more than a business; it became a classroom. In the back, workshops hummed with energy: how to use a sewing machine, how to budget, how to run a kitchen.

They weren't just working now, they were training, teaching, building something that would outlast any handout.

And the people who once stood in food lines?

Now they stood behind counters, registers, and real businesses.

The model spread and the mayor did get re-elected!

One district turned into two. Then five. Neighborhoods changed. Families once sleeping under overpasses moved into apartments rebuilt by the very people living in them. We watched as a community-run café opened, a struggling family moved into their first real apartment, and a group of residents pooled money to buy a van they turned into a ride-share.

Word spread beyond Italy, with each country adapting community-led initiatives that fit their needs.

In Kenya, the model shifted to the fields. Farmers used micro-loans to start cooperatives, inspired by projects like One Acre Fund, which helps small-scale farmers access financing and training.

In Brazil, community leaders launched housing programs that transformed favelas into livable communities, following the footsteps of organizations like Minha Casa Minha Vida, a government program aimed at providing low-income housing.

In India, a rideshare initiative connected job-seekers with work in growing industries, similar to efforts led by the Selco Foundation, which promotes solar-powered rickshaw services for low-income drivers.

To amplify the impact, we connected with Muhammad Yunus, the pioneer of microfinance, and partnered with organizations like Grameen Bank, which had already lifted millions out of poverty by offering small business loans.

Ellie nudged me. "So, global poverty solved?"

I opened my mouth to answer, but The Reminder stepped out with a traditional Italian cappuccino in hand. "Nice work but don't slow down."

A few seconds later, the portal flared open behind us, scooping us up like a cosmic vacuum cleaner.

THREE

−2080−

THE LAST CRUMB

SDG 2: Zero Hunger

T he moment I landed, my tongue felt like sandpaper as my skin prickled with heat.

"Hot, hot, too hot!" Ellie yelled beside me, already face-planted into the cracked earth. "Tell me we landed in a sauna."

We had not landed in a sauna.

We had landed in Lagos, Nigeria, or what was left of it.

The city, once a booming hub of energy and life, had crumbled into a skeletal ruin. The Third Mainland Bridge sagged, its supports looking like overcooked spaghetti barely holding themselves together. Streets that were once gridlocked with honking cars and shouting vendors now stretched empty, swallowed by dust and silence, except for the occasional rustle of a starving rat.

Overhead, the sky was a sickly yellow, like the sun had clocked out early, officially giving up on the disaster below.

A massive sign, its edges burnt and tattered, flapped weakly in the hot breeze:

RATION: 1 MEAL PER WEEK.

Ellie sat up, blinking at the sign. "Okay, this is worse than 2050."

A skeletal child tugged at my sleeve, "mister, do you have food?"

My throat tightened. I opened my mouth, but nothing came out.

Another child begged me for a coin to put in the crumb machine to buy a crumb. Ellie and I turned our pockets inside out desperately searching for coins but didn't have any.

The Reminder appeared beside us, this time as a starving boy, ribs poking out of his skin.

"You must find a way to prevent this from happening."

The shimmer appeared as the past was calling us back.

We had to stop this before it ever happened.

The world blurred, and we were pulled backward—

Back to 2025.

FOUR

– 2 0 2 5 –

I DIDN'T MEAN TO
START A FOOD FIGHT

SDG 2: Zero Hunger

I landed hard in the middle of Ikoyi, Lagos, a place known for its wealth and high-end living.

Ellie crashed down beside me, screaming, "okay, I'm filing a complaint with whatever cosmic force is handling this trip! Can we get at least one First Class landing?"

Instead of stifling heat and starvation, the air was thick with something else, roasted meat, fresh bread, and spices. Laughter echoed around us. People in designer suits and flowing gowns moved between massive banquet tables, their plates overflowing with food.

We were at a feast, a ridiculously expensive, absurdly over-the-top feast.

Ellie stared at a golden roasted turkey the size of a small dog. "Leyth... are we still in the right timeline?"

The Reminder appeared next to us, this time as a man in a velvet suit, swirling a glass of wine. "Oh, you're in the right place. Welcome to the problem."

I was confused, "this doesn't look like starvation."

The Reminder pointed, "look closer."

In the distance, kids from wealthy families were having an all-out food fight, hurling slices of cake at each other while servants stacked trays of untouched gourmet dishes into bins. A mansion made entirely of chocolate stood at the edge of a garden, where a fountain spewed liquid gold caramel instead of water.

A waiter wove between the tables, collecting untouched plates of lobster, caviar, and truffle pasta, and dumping them straight into a trash bin.

Further ahead, I saw trucks loaded with mountains of food drive away... straight to a landfill near Mile 12 Market.

Meanwhile, just outside the Eko Hotel banquet hall, I caught glimpses of workers in stiff uniforms, standing at the corners of the building, their hands clasped tightly to their empty stomachs.

The Reminder's form shifted into a young girl in tattered clothes, clutching her empty stomach. "Just a few streets away, thousands of children are starving. And remember what I told you about redistribution."

Ellie scowled, "this is unbelievable!"

I took a deep breath, "alright. We're shifting things around."

Follow the Waste

I slipped away from the banquet and into the alley behind the kitchens. I couldn't miss the endless row of dumpsters lining the back wall, overflowing with perfectly edible food. At the top were rats, their tiny paws digging into the mess, feasting on torn bread rolls, pasta slick with sauce, and overripe fruit split open. And beyond the dumpsters? People were hungry, desperate.

They were picking through the trash, filling their bags with whatever wasn't too ruined to eat.

Ellie grabbed my arm, "it's not like there isn't enough food to go around."

I nodded, "yeah, you're right. We need to redistribute some of this wasted food to the people out there who need it."

We marched straight back inside.

We found the catering manager, a man with a too-tight tie and an expression that said he'd rather be anywhere else.

"Hey," I said, flashing my best 'I know what I'm talking about' smile. "You guys throw out a lot of food, right?"

His frown deepened. "That's... not really your concern."

"Oh, but it is." I pulled out a tablet (okay, fine, I borrowed it from an unattended table). "Because restaurants and hotels that donate excess food get massive tax breaks. And if you partner with shelters and food banks, you don't just save money, you look like heroes."

Ellie leaned in. "Big PR win. Customers love supporting businesses that do good."

The manager blinked. He studied the numbers on my screen. Then, he slowly nodded.

"We... might be able to make this work, and maybe I can get a promotion!"

The Future Shifts

Food that once rotted in dumpsters was now filling plates instead of landfills. What started as a local initiative spread worldwide. Major restaurant chains, hotel franchises, and grocery stores joined forces to prevent food waste. Second Bite, a global app, connected surplus meals to shelters, food banks, and community kitchens. Governments passed new policies incentivizing food donations. The once-overflowing trash bins? Nearly empty. And for the first time, hunger wasn't just being fought, it was being outsmarted.

The Reminder, now appearing as a woman ladling soup for a long line of people, smiled.

"One meal at a time."

The veil of light surrounded us again.

Ellie huffed, "oh no, I'm not ready to leave just yet!"

But within seconds, we were hurled forward in time—

Straight into 2095.

FIVE

-2095-

THE BIG APPLE TURNED ROTTEN

SDG 3: Good Health & Well-being

I hit the ground hard—again. Asphalt scraped against my palms. At this point, I was convinced time travel had it out for me.

Ellie whined beside me, rubbing her elbow. "If we don't get a soft landing at least once, I'm suing the universe."

We looked up and immediately wished we hadn't.

We were in New York City, but not the one from postcards and movies. The skyline still had its famous giants. The Empire State Building loomed to our right, now overshadowed by monstrous LED billboards. One World Trade Center still cut through the clouds, but the streets below?

Absolute chaos.

Sluggish, pale-eyed people shuffled around, their bodies bloated in unnatural ways. One guy had an arm so swollen it looked like a sausage casing ready to burst. Another man had fingers permanently coated in neon-orange cheese dust from eating so many cheetos. No, seriously, the dust WAS his fingers. A woman sat on a bench, sipping a soda through a straw that led straight to her stomach like an IV tube. On the opposite side, a woman and her daughter sat on another bench, slurping from two oversized, glittery cups—one neon purple and the other one electric orange. The drinks fizzed and glowed like unstable science experiments, and I swear, their skin was beginning to tint to match.

Ellie squinted at a kid waddling past, his entire torso shaped like a chicken nugget. "Uh...is that guy okay?"

The Reminder appeared beside us, flickering between an overworked doctor, a frustrated fitness instructor, and a concerned nutritionist.... Its voice was grim. "No, and neither is anyone else."

As we walked, I caught sight of a man slumped against a graffiti-covered bench in Madison Square Park. His body was so puffed up like a marshmallow, he couldn't even bend his body to sit down. Not far off, a boy was chasing his little brother through the street, yelling, "give it back!" The younger brother clutched a bulging bag of rainbow-colored candies, giggling like a madman. With every piece they popped into their mouths, their skin changed—one was going lime green, the other cherry red. They looked less like humans and more like a pair of rogue M&Ms.

One guy waddled past us with a body shaped like a massive, soggy French fry. I mean, crispy on the outside, mushy on the inside. He blinked at me slowly, ketchup oozing from the corners of his eyes. A group of children sat on the steps of an abandoned subway entrance. Instead of playing, they mindlessly chewed on brightly colored snack cubes, their faces devoid of energy. One kid hiccupped, and his tongue flashed blue like a malfunctioning LED.

Ellie nudged me, "this is freaky!"

I couldn't believe my eyes, "I know, I'm in complete shock."

As if I was coming out of a trance, I slowly patted Ellie on the back.

"Alright. Let's take the junk out of food."

SIX

-2025-

SNACK WARS

SDG 3: Good Health & Well-being

We landed, miraculously on our feet this time, in the middle of a bustling New York City sidewalk.

"Okay," Ellie said, turning in a circle. "Now this is more like it."

Everything seemed normal.

No human Cheetos. No nugget-shaped torsos.

Taxis honked, dodging jaywalkers. Food carts smoked on the corners. Billboards blinked ads for movies, gadgets, and one disturbingly glittery ad that read:

"NOW IN SCHOOLS: Junk food vending machines bringing you your Daily Dose of ChocoFriedCheez."

Ellie stared. "Okay, that sounds really gross."

Then a guy in a donut costume tackled me.

"FREE SAMPLES!" he shrieked, hurling a bag of glowing

orange and pink donuts into my hands before vanishing into a crowd.

I turned to Ellie, who now held a plastic tray of "Slurp-N-Go Nacho Smoothies."

She gagged.

I gagged.

The Reminder appeared beside us, this time as a nurse overwhelmed with paperwork. "You need to get people to care about their health and about real food...before it's too late."

We had no time to waste. So we quickly looked around us and rallied a dream team: a local chef, a squad of concerned moms, and a bunch of high schoolers tired of getting mystery-orange fingerprints from neon cheese dust.

After hours of deliberating, we decided to launch The Great Snack Swap:

One table displayed processed junk: glowing slurpees, fried sugar cubes, "chicken-flavored foam bites."

The other table offered the real deal: frozen yogurt pops with berries, sweet potato chips, hummus wraps, air-popped popcorn with herbs, and watermelon smoothies.

We blindfolded taste-testers, thousands of them.

Thousands gathered, curious and buzzing with excitement. We blindfolded taste-testers from all walks of life, and even the most devoted junk-food fans chose real food—by taste alone. Phones were everywhere; people started filming the challenge, posting videos to social media in real time. "I swear I just had the best dessert," one guy mumbled after tasting yogurt with honey and chia seeds. "But... like, the healthy kind."

We invited TikTok foodies and health influencers to host a live event: Junk vs. Real: Taste Test Throwdown.

Teenagers judged.

Junk lost.

That's when things went *viral*.

Local news stations caught wind of our taste tests. TikTok lit up.

Billboards changed overnight:

"Keep it real. Ditch the junk."

"Your body called. It wants its veggies."

We worked with chefs to bring real food back into schools and community centers.

Into backpacks went trail mix, dried mango, almond butter packets, mini veggie wraps, and chilled fruit juice boxes. Kids started trading apple slices at recess like Pokémon cards. Lunch trays featured fruit kabobs instead of shrink-wrapped beige blobs.

One 8th grader squealed, "OMG! I love hummus!"

Ellie leaned against a lamppost, watching two kids race each other to a fountain, splashing in the water like they had no idea the world had almost turned them into junk-food-mutant-creatures.

I let out a breath. "I think we did it."

Across the park, The Reminder, now a silver-haired grand-mother in running shoes and a sun visor, sat on a bench, watching a group of teenagers peel an orange and split a banana.

She smiled. "You gave them their health back."

I turned to Ellie. "You ever notice how saving the world always involves way more running than we do in basketball?"

Ellie flopped dramatically onto a park bench. "At least in bas-ketball, we have softer landings."

And then, as always, the shimmer returned.

Time for our next mission.

SEVEN

–2110–

WELCOME TO THE
WORLD OF ILLITERACY

SDG 4: Quality Education

Down I went again, like a bad rerun.

Seriously, was it too much to ask for one dignified landing?

Ellie murmured next to me, face down in the dirt.

"If I get a concussion from time travel, I'm—"

"I know, I know," I cut her off as I pushed myself upright. "You're suing the universe."

She groaned in agreement, spitting dust.

I looked up, taking in the eerie silence around us.

We were in Helsinki, Finland—

Or at least, what was left of it.

It should have been a city of learning, innovation, and

world-class schools.

Instead, we had landed in the world's most depressing library clearance sale.

Schools stood empty, their windows boarded up like haunted houses for ghost teachers. Books lay in the streets, untouched and collecting dust, as if reading had gone extinct. Signs were plastered on old universities: "Learning is history!"

Even the Oodi Library, once a beacon of modern education, was chained shut like it had committed a crime.

The city's famous trams still glided along, but there were no students clutching textbooks, no kids running late to class. Even the street performers in Senate Square looked...more clueless.

Ellie pointed at a billboard featuring a Finnish influencer wearing sunglasses and holding a smoothie.

"WHO NEEDS BOOKS WHEN YOU CAN WATCH VIDEOS? STAY ENTERTAINED, NOT EDUCATED!"

Ellie turned to me, horrified.

"They commercialized ignorance. This is worse than the time my WiFi went out for six hours."

The Reminder appeared beside us, this time as an old, frail teacher clutching a broken chalkboard like a lifeline.

"They gave up on formal education," she sighed.

We stepped inside what used to be a classroom. The walls were covered in peeling posters about algebra and grammar, like fossils from a time when people actually knew what 'hypotenuse' meant.

Before I could say anything, a voice interrupted behind us. "Mitä sinä teet täällä?" ("What are you doing here?") We spun around to see an elderly Finnish man in a thick wool sweater, holding a cup of steaming kahvi (coffee). His bushy eyebrows furrowed as he looked us up and down.

Ellie, ever the smooth talker, attempted diplomacy.

"Uh... koulut ovat..." She glanced at me, "what's the word for 'gone'?"

I shrugged, "poof?"

The man sighed, mumbling something that definitely sounded like an insult, and took a sip of his coffee.

"You are tourists?"

I considered lying, but given the man's piercing gaze, I figured honesty was the way to go.

"We're trying to fix education. Any chance you know what happened?"

He took a long sip of his kahvi, the kind of dramatic pause only a seasoned teacher could pull off. Then he nodded solemnly.

"Everyone got into social media. So they got rid of schools and books."

For a moment, he just stared into his coffee, like he was looking back at a whole world that had slipped away.

"I used to be a teacher," he said quietly. "This was my school. Every day, I come here, just to remember."

Ellie frowned. "What happened?"

The man looked up with tears in his eyes, "Social media made more money than schools and universities, so they shut us down. Teenagers like you started spending their days on social media instead. Formal education went out of style. Even bookstores closed down."

A chill ran down my spine. No school? No books? That was like... canceling oxygen.

As if on cue, a former professor-turned barista at the café across the street shouted in frustration:

"Lukekaa kirjaa tai ostakaa kahvia!" ("Read a book if you want to be served coffee at my café!")

We walked over to the café. A few customers sat at tables, halfheartedly flipping open books, squinting at the pages like they were ancient relics. Apparently, the coffee was so good that

31

pretending to read had become the price of admission. In the corner, a guy held an algebra textbook upside down, nodding as if he totally understood it.

Ellie stared at him. "Okay, but... can we talk about how no one actually knows how to read anymore?"

The barista paused, "oh, some people do. But literacy? That is a luxury skill now."

I didn't like the sound of that.

A minute later, a businessman walked in trying to order a sandwich by yelling emojis at the cashier:

"BREAD. MEAT. SMILEY FACE. LIGHTNING BOLT."

The barista looked very unimpressed. "Sir, we don't accept spoken emoji—"

Instead of answering, the businessman just grinned and gave a giant thumbs-up.

I turned to the barista, "do people seriously communicate in emojis now?"

He shrugged and nodded toward a digital billboard flashing outside the window — a giant clapping hands emoji next to a diploma.

In bold letters, it blared:

"BOOKS ARE A THING OF THE PAST! KEEP UP WITH THE FUTURE AND JUST MEMORIZE OUR FUN SYMBOL SYSTEM!"

Ellie pulled my arm, panic rising in her voice, "Leyth, this is insane! Now, I regret ever complaining when my mother nagged me to read every day!"

The Reminder materialized beside us, this time looking way more stressed than usual, flipping through a thick instruction manual labeled, "How to Rebuild Literacy When People Think Words are a Waste of Time."

Just then, a man sprinted past the café, waving a completely blank piece of paper in the air. "I FOUND A SECRET MESSAGE! BUT I CAN'T READ IT!"

Ellie clapped a hand to her forehead, "we're doomed."

An elderly man sitting next to us with a blank book in hand, took another slow sip of his coffee. "This is Finland. Strange things happen. We just drink our coffee and enjoy the fresh air. It keeps us balanced."

But there was no balance in all of this.

This was chaos.

And if we didn't act fast, entire generations would lose the ability to communicate on a more intellectual level.

I suddenly felt motivated again. "Alright, I've seen enough. Let's get our education and books back."

EIGHT

–2025–

I DIDN'T MEAN TO
LAND ON A GRANDMA

SDG 4: Quality Education

We were sucked back into 2025, in time to save education, one stolen chalkboard at a time.

I braced for impact, but this time, miracle of miracles, I landed on something soft.

"Hey," I whispered. "This isn't bad."

Then the soft thing screamed and flung me off.

A small Finnish grandmother was glaring at me from behind a massive knitting project.

"Anteeksi! Sorry!" I scrambled to my feet, realizing I had landed on grandma knitting in a very normal café. People were reading newspapers. Kids were actually doing homework. No emoji-speaking businessmen.

I looked out the window. Down the street, a public school stood, but it was falling apart—half the windows were cracked, and the paint peeled like an ancient artifact. A handwritten sign read:

"LESS MATH, MORE TIK TOK VIDEOS!"

The Reminder appeared next to me, now dressed as a tired-looking principal.

"This is where it began," The Reminder said. "Schools died out because students started replacing reading and writing with social media scrolling."

Just as The Reminder finished his sentence, a teenager strutted past us, holding her phone at the perfect selfie angle, totally unaware that she almost walked straight into a mop bucket.

She giggled, snapped a pouty photo, and said to no one in particular, "ugh, who even needs lectures when your Instagram pics get more likes than a professor?"

That's when the idea hit. Not a thunderbolt kind of idea.

"Okay," I said slowly, eyes widening. "What if we recruit social media influencers to make education look like the next big trend?"

Ellie wasn't sure she heard me correctly, "influencers?"

I nodded. "Yeah. If they can make iced coffee and lip balm go viral, why not Shakespeare?"

She crossed her arms. "I actually hate how much sense that makes."

The Reminder popped up beside us, now looking like a fashion blogger with thick-rimmed glasses. "Make reading cool again!" she said, posing with a stack of textbooks like they were Gucci handbags.

#TeachTok Begins

We started with one: a makeup influencer who secretly loved Shakespeare. She posted a dramatic reading of *Macbeth* while face contouring like her life depended on it. It got 2 million views in a day.

Then a gaming YouTuber broke down algebra using sports stats.

Soon we had science teachers doing slime experiments on live streams while history buffs reenacted ancient battles with Minecraft mods. Even an economics professor did a dance challenge called #SupplyAndDemandShuffle.

We launched a campaign—#TeachTok.

Tagline: "If you can scroll it, you can learn it."

It blew up.

The best part? Teachers weren't just back—they were *famous*. Some of them had more followers than influencers.

A chemistry teacher known only as "Ms. Boom" now had merch and her own channel where she exploded things and explained molecules in the same breath.

And kids?

They were watching.

News outlets picked it up immediately. Hashtags exploded.

Teachers walked into classrooms with cameras and whiteboards. Kids walked in with questions. Libraries unlocked their doors. And for the first time in years, learning was trending.

We visited Oodi Library a week later.

It wasn't just open, it was packed.

Kids sat in beanbags with books cracked open. One group huddled around a teacher who was livestreaming a math trick with a Rubik's Cube. Upstairs, someone ran a creative writing workshop on how to turn fanfiction into thesis-driven essays.

Ellie stood next to me, arms crossed but clearly proud. "Well," she said, "we made education go viral. What's next, solving traffic?"

Before I could answer, the air shimmered. Uh-oh.

The Reminder appeared beside us in a hoodie that said "Keep

Education Alive" while he sipped coffee from a mug shaped like a giant pencil.

"You reminded them that education is cool."

"Yeah," I said. "Turns out, people just needed a reminder."

A second later, the wind started swirling, the familiar pull of the portal.

I turned to Ellie. "Another crisis down."

She quickly responded, "and fourteen more to go. Do any of them involve pizza?"

And then the portal opened wide, glowing like someone had supercharged a hologram with fireworks. It scooped us up like a cosmic vacuum cleaner.

Onward, into the next mission.

NINE

-2125-

WHERE DID ALL THE WOMEN GO?

SDG 5: Gender Equality

I was flung onto a marble floor, which, lucky for me, was polished to a mirror-like shine.

Unfortunately, that meant I skidded across it like a human air hockey puck before stopping face-first at the base of a podium.

Ellie, because she's somehow immune to time-travel whiplash, stood up, dusted off her t-shirt, and giggled, "you need to work on those landings, pal."

I moaned, "next time, you go first."

We looked around. The Cairo International Conference Center stretched before us—massive, sleek, and suspiciously lopsided.

Rows of businessmen in stiff suits filled one side of the room, whispering deals, exchanging handshakes, and nodding way too seriously. The other side?

Practically empty.

I frowned. "Where is everyone?"

The Reminder appeared beside us, this time as a woman in a sharp navy blue blazer.

Ellie nudged me, "why does this place feel so odd?"

The Reminder gestured toward the filled seats. "Look closer."

I examined the crowd and my eyes shocked me.

It was all men.

There were no women. They looked like clones out of The Matrix, all in black suits, moving and nodding in unison.

Ellie seemed confused. "Where are all the women? Time to shake things up!"

The Reminder nodded. And just like that, the shimmer surrounded us again.

TEN

−2025−

BALANCING THE SCALES

SDG 5: Gender Equality

I was jolted mid-stride into a modern office, nearly tripping over my own feet as sunlight ricocheted off the endless glass. The Cairo Business District stretched around us, a maze of steel towers shimmering in the heat. The air was thick with the scent of fresh mint tea and car exhaust.

Before I could react, Ellie grabbed my sleeve and yanked me behind a row of very expensive-looking leather chairs. "Leyth, hide—corporate villains, twelve o'clock."

Sure enough, a boardroom full of executives sat at a polished mahogany table, debating salaries like they were trading stocks.

A guy with a ridiculous gold tie leaned forward, tapping a pen against his Oumda coffee mug. "We could raise wages, but why bother? The numbers show we can keep them lower for women, and they still take the jobs."

Another man chuckled. "Exactly. And leadership roles? We all know who's best suited for those."

The Reminder, now appearing as a sharp suited male executive with a briefcase, whispered, "show them, Ellie, that women are equally capable."

The Switcheroo

Ten minutes later, Ellie disappeared into the supply closet.

She emerged as Eli—hair tucked into a cap, sleeves rolled, blazer one size too big.

She strutted into the boardroom like she owned it. I followed her lead, trying not to trip over my own confidence.

Gold Tie Guy looked up. "You are?"

"Es-Salāmo ʿalaykom! Gentlemen! I'm Eli from Masr Capital. Thought I'd observe. Might invest."

She said it like she wasn't lying through her teeth.

They welcomed her like royalty.

For the next hour, "Eli" ran circles around them, pitching:

- A vertical expansion strategy into underserved regional markets, backed by demographic data.
- Restructuring their supply chain to reduce operational costs by 18% over two fiscal quarters.
- A new client retention model based on predictive analytics, aimed at boosting quarterly revenue by 12%.
- And the kicker: a profitability forecast showing how firms with more diverse decision-making styles consistently outperform monolithic leadership teams in volatile markets.

The men nodded, impressed. "Smart guy," one whispered. "What's his name?"

Then Ellie yanked off the cap. The ponytail came down.

Gold Tie Guy's eyes went wide.

"You're a—"

"Girl?" she finished. "Yup. And I just bossed every one of you in your own game."

The Reminder almost fell off of his chair laughing. "Now that's a performance."

Women in Leadership

It started with a moment.

One woman. One mic. One room full of people who didn't expect her to speak up.

But she did.

And the internet listened.

The video went viral.

Clips flooded social media.

Headlines lit up.

Hashtags trended:

#SheBelongsHere

#HireHerAlready

Wage transparency laws were passed in record time.

Equal parental leave became the new normal, not just a perk.

Schools across Cairo launched Girls in Tech programs—because coding isn't just for boys.

Women of every background led discussions, pitched solutions, and signed deals. This wasn't just inclusion. This was a major transformation.

The Reminder, now a young girl at the podium clutching a notepad, looked at us and smiled.

"You didn't just open doors," she said. "You reminded the world why they should never have been closed."

Ellie beamed.
Just then, the shimmer returned.
A flash of light. A whoosh of wind.

ELEVEN

–2130–

I HOPE YOU LIKE DEHYDRATION

SDG 6: Clean Water and Sanitation

I slammed face-first into something wet and slimy.

"Ughh—what even is this?" I gagged, scrambling upright. "This better be mud and not some kind of mutant jellyfish."

Ellie landed beside me.

I wiped my face and looked around. That's when my stomach dropped.

Toronto was unrecognizable.

The streets reeked. The sewage system was out of control. Gutters overflowed with a foul, brown grime that trickled past sandbags like it was trying to escape the city. Tap water was so rusted and unsafe, people had stopped drinking it. Instead, they scraped together whatever they could to buy bottled water, which

45

cost more than some people's weekly wage. A cracked vending machine stood on the corner, its sign flickering: "Water Sold Out."

"Wow, I really took clean water and good sanitation for granted!" Ellie gasped.

The Reminder appeared beside us, this time in a cracked hazmat suit with a limp Canadian flag patch peeling off the arm. She looked like she'd walked through a disaster zone.

"It's only going to get worse," she warned, voice muffled behind her foggy visor. "People are already fighting over ice cubes sold at supermarkets."

I gasped, "what happened?"

She didn't sugarcoat it. "People wasted a lot of water. They left taps running for long periods of time. Some took at least five showers a day and even bathed in bottled water. Businesses used drinking water to power fountains in corporate offices and hotel lobbies. This was on top of climate change melting glaciers, evaporating rivers and drying up everything. She then gestured at the billboard for bottled Maple Supreme water. "Look, a bottle is so expensive you'd think it was made of liquid gold!"

Ellie pointed toward a smelly sewage drain. "What about sanitation?"

The Reminder pinched her nose. "Gone. Pipes dried out in many communities, causing sanitation systems to break down when the water stopped flowing."

Ellie turned to me, "please tell me we can save our water supply."

I exhaled, "let's just hope we're not too late."

And that was the cue for the shimmer to take us back in time to fix the flow.

TWELVE

–2025–

THE WATER WAR BEGINS

SDG 6: Clean Water and Sanitation

I crashed onto a cold, polished floor, which, compared to my usual landings, was practically a luxury.

Ellie quickly looked around. "Did we finally land in a place where people own chairs?"

We had. It was a very expensive looking place, actually.

We were in Toronto, inside a swanky gala hall filled with Canada's richest and most hydrated citizens. Floor-to-ceiling windows overlooked the CN Tower, twinkling against the night sky. Crystal chandeliers reflected the glow of absurdly overpriced centerpieces made entirely out of bottled water.

Yes, bottled water centerpieces.

Each table had bottles of glacier runoff, iceberg melt, Maple Supreme water.

I tried to blend in with the crowd. Ellie, meanwhile, was already on the lookout for water wastage.

"Hey," she nudged me, pointing at the buffet. "Is that a fountain with sparkling water over there?"

I turned, and, sure enough, in the middle of the ballroom was a gold-plated, three-tiered fountain gushing sparking water.

"I... I don't know what I expected, but this is bizarre," I whispered.

The Reminder appeared beside us, disguised as a sharply dressed woman carrying a clipboard. "You can still stop the water crisis from occurring," she said dryly. "

She gestured toward a group of business executives in tailored suits sipping sparkling water and casually discussing how to charge people more.

One man, adjusting his cufflinks, snorted, "the more exclusive we make the bottled water, the more they'll pay."

"ARE YOU SERIOUS?!" I shouted.

The entire room turned to stare at me.

Ellie coughed. "Well, that's one way to make an entrance."

A waiter carrying a massive platter of butter tarts nearly tripped over himself in shock. Someone shrieked, "oh my sweet poutine!" — or something just as dramatic.

I had exactly three seconds before security started escorting me out. So, naturally, I went for Plan B: Unleash maximum chaos.

I grabbed a silver platter from a passing waiter, scooped up a stack of fancy pancakes, and flung them like frisbees toward the greedy water hoarders.

SPLAT.

Pure Canadian pandemonium erupted.

One guy got a face full of syrup and stumbled backward into a tower of bottled water, which immediately collapsed on him. He yelled under the pile, arms flailing. Before he could even react, half the room rushed over, not to help him, but to grab those precious bottles off his chest.

A table flipped over, sending smoked salmon flying. A woman screamed, "MY DESIGNER GOOSE-FEATHER COAT!" as she was hit with a pancake. Someone else yelled, "the water! Grab me a bottle!" like it was the most valuable thing in the room (which, honestly, it might have been).

Ellie, dodged a flying crème brûlée tart.

Meanwhile, I sprinted toward the mic stand at the front of the room.

"ATTENTION EVERYONE," I shouted. "STOP TRYING TO SELL WATER LIKE IT'S A LUXURY ITEM."

Security stormed the stage.

Time to go.

The Hockey Disaster

We burst out of the gala, guards hot on our heels.

Ellie glanced over her shoulder. "Uh, problem. They don't look happy."

"Gee, you think?" I huffed. "Maybe they're upset about the syrup tsunami."

I had no idea where we were going. But Toronto was full of underground walkways and hockey rinks every five blocks, so naturally, we did the worst possible thing:

We ran into a building without looking.

Big mistake.

I skidded to a halt. Bright lights. Cheering. The sharp chill of ice in the air.

We were standing at center ice of a professional hockey game.

The entire Scotiabank Arena crowd stared at us.

One of the hockey players skated over, tapping his stick. "Uh…

kids? You're not supposed to be here."

The announcer's voice echoed through the speakers:

"Uh... folks, we have... two random teens on the ice? I don't think they're on the roster."

I turned to Ellie, "why do we always end up in the worst possible places?"

Before he could answer, the security guards from the gala stormed in through the tunnels.

"THERE THEY ARE!"

The hockey players immediately misread the situation.

One of them skated over, cracking his knuckles through his gloves. "Oh, you wanna go? You wanna drop the gloves?!"

Another grinned, smacking his stick against the ice. "I respect the commitment, but this is a weird time for tryouts."

Ellie held up her hands. "Nope, nope, definitely not here to fight or try out."

Too late.

The ref skated up, looking mildly amused. "Well, you're here, and we've already got a crowd... might as well make it interesting."

The puck dropped.

The crowd ROARED.

And suddenly, I was being chased across the ice by a 6'4" enforcer who clearly thought I had challenged him.

Ellie dodged a bodycheck, slid past a goalie, and somehow ended up on a Zamboni.

"THIS IS THE GREATEST DAY OF MY LIFE!" she screamed.

We sprinted off the ice, still ducking security guards and angry hockey fans. Ellie dove into the nearest hallway, yanked open a door, and pulled me into—

A luxury hotel bathroom.

Like, chandeliers-above-the-sinks level luxury.

I couldn't believe my eyes. "What is this place?"

Ellie pointed to the sign. "Apparently, the Spritz. And apparently, they don't believe in quick showers—look at this!"

I peeked into one of the stalls. Not a single water-saving nozzle in sight. Just deep, steaming bathtubs, like each guest needed to recreate Niagara Falls nightly.

"Who needs that much water to wash?" I asked, staring at a tub big enough to bathe a walrus.

The Reminder walked in behind us, now dressed as a Toronto utility worker with a patch that read "FLOW Control." She sighed and gestured toward the city skyline visible through the bathroom window.

"People left the tap running while brushing their teeth, filled swimming pools every weekend, watered lawns during droughts—and now?" Her voice dropped. "The city's drying out."

I followed her gesture. The CN Tower pierced the sky like a giant needle.

And then it hit me.

"Wait—Ellie," I grabbed her arm. "I've got an idea!"

"Oh no," she said. "I know that look."

I didn't answer. I was already running.

We sprinted through downtown Toronto, dodging cyclists, food trucks, and a man walking six poodles in matching raincoats. Up the elevator, past the stunned tourists, straight to the top of the CN Tower.

From up there, you could see everything. The lakes. The lawns. The fountains. The problem.

I grabbed the emergency announcement mic from a shocked tour guide.

"Toronto," I said, my voice echoing through speakers across the city, "we need to talk about your water."

"Here's the deal," I shouted. "We're not here to shame you for bathing ... well, maybe a little ... but we *are* here to stop water from becoming extinct."

From our perch at the top of the CN Tower, the city unfolded beneath us—skyscrapers, gardens, fountains, and hundreds of parched-looking rooftops. But it wasn't just the view that gave us an edge. Down below, we'd landed right next to one of the city's busiest intersections, surrounded by government offices, banks, and the kind of important-looking people who always seem to be rushing around with lattes and very urgent emails.

We pitched the simplest idea first:

"For every gallon saved, you earn a tax deduction. Conserve water, save money. Waste it? Pay more."

We even had a name for it: The Drip Credit.

Within minutes, curious passersby gathered beneath the tower's loudspeakers. Some looked up. Others pulled out their phones. A few government officials stepped onto the plaza below, phones already pressed to their ears. One guy in a pinstripe suit raised a coffee cup to make a toast.

Then the press arrived.

A couple of reporters showed up with their microphones, peppering us with questions. That evening we watched ourselves on national television!

Within days, companies started gamifying the idea of water conservation. Offices started monthly water-saving competitions: teams tracked their usage, posted updates in break rooms, and celebrated wins with shoutouts and rewards.

Restaurants gave "Water Warrior" discounts to customers who brought their own reusable bottles.

Even hockey arenas got involved, replacing old equipment with smart systems that reused melted rink ice to reduce waste.

Between the maple syrup war and the hockey rink fiasco, we'd gotten enough media attention to expose the water crisis.

Two months later, the city looked different.

The fountains were sensible.

People started swapping long baths for quick showers.

Shower timers became a thing. Some households even turned it into a family challenge: who could wash fastest without freezing?

The public parks were green again—actually green, not that crunchy beige that used to pretend to be grass.

And the sewage system?

For the first time in years, water flowed steadily through the pipes again. Not perfectly, but it moved.

This wasn't just about infrastructure.

It was about awareness—spreading, shifting, becoming a habit.

Best part? Water (including the bottled kind) was back to being affordable for everyone.

Ellie and I toasted our success with biodegradable cups of tap water (filtered, obviously).

Of course since we were in Canada we had to visit a Tim Hortons and try their donuts.

Ellie held up a Boston Cream. "OMG, you have to try this."

I took a bite. It was heavenly.

"Okay," I admitted. "I'd time travel just for this."

Ellie jumped up. "So, what's next?"

I sighed, brushing a smudge of syrup off my jacket.

"Hopefully something that doesn't involve me getting body-checked by a giant hockey player!"

THIRTEEN

–2110–

THE ENERGY CRISIS

SDG 7: Affordable and Clean Energy

I met the ground with bone-jarring force, which, at this point, was nothing new.

What *was* new was the fact that I immediately smacked into something cold and metallic.

Ellie was somewhere behind me. "I swear, if we've been dumped onto another pile of scrap metal, I'm quitting this mission."

I sat up, blinking at the complete and utter darkness.

No neon billboards. No glowing storefronts. No AI-powered traffic lights flashing confusing signals at pedestrians. Just a dead, silent city.

Ellie waved a hand in front of his face. "Ugh, is it just me, or is Beijing missing its entire power grid?"

A gust of wind howled through the abandoned streets. The buildings were dark, their once-bright windows shattered and dark. People huddled around small fire pits, some desperate for warmth, others seeking light to read.

It looked like the world had run out of energy and everyone had just... given up.

"This is Beijing?" I asked, my voice barely above a whisper.

The Reminder stood beside us, this time as a frazzled scientist with wild hair and an empty coffee cup.

"Welcome to the blackout," she said heavily.

Ellie looked at a dead billboard that used to flash AI-generated luxury ads. "Okay, but... did nobody think of inventing a backup generator?"

The Reminder gestured toward a giant coal plant in the distance, or what was left of it. The cooling towers had crumbled. Smoke stacks lay in ruins. Even the emergency lights had given up on life.

"Fossil fuels ran out," she continued. "And instead of transitioning to clean energy *before* that happened, people waited. Then it was too late."

I shivered. "So, what? The entire world is just... permanently unplugged?"

The Reminder pointed to an electric sedan abandoned in the middle of the road. Someone had carved the word "USELESS" into the side.

"Transportation failed. Factories stopped. There's no power to run hospitals, schools, or even water purification plants."

Ellie whistled, "wow...so, basically, the planet quit."

The Reminder regretfully agreed, "pretty much."

I squared my shoulders. "Then it's high time we did something about it."

A thick fog of light surrounded us.

And we were yanked back—

FOURTEEN

–2025–

WHO UNPLUGGED THE WORLD?

SDG 7: Affordable and Clean Energy

We landed mid-stride on a chaotic street in Beijing, and I mean *chaotic*.

Neon signs blinked in every direction. Self-driving delivery vans zoomed by like they were on fire. Electric rickshaws beeped furiously.

I barely avoided getting flattened by one before Ellie yanked me back.

"Hey buddy," she said, "maybe work on your landings?"

I brushed myself off. "Well, at least the lights are still on."

The skyline glittered with solar-paneled skyscrapers. Wind turbines spun along the rooftops. Roads hummed with electric traffic.

At first glance, the future looked flawless.

But then, of course, Ellie disappeared.

"Ellie?" I spun in place. No answer.

Right on cue, The Reminder appeared, this time dressed as a city planner holding blueprints like ancient scrolls.

"You lost your friend again," she said, completely unfazed.

"WHERE did she go this time?!"

The Reminder pointed toward a tall mirrored building behind us.

The sign read:

BEIJING SMART GRID CONTROL CENTER

(*Authorized Personnel Only*)

"Oh no," I gasped.

Ellie and the Button That Changed Everything

Inside the command center, Ellie was doing what Ellie does best:

Touching things she should absolutely *not* be touching.

She had somehow wandered past security, tripped over a server cable, and accidentally opened the control panel for Beijing's entire renewable energy network.

She stared at the blinking touchscreen. "Ooooh, shiny interface."

Before I could stop her, she tapped a button labeled:

"System-Wide Diagnostics Override"

The lights went out.

The Six-Hour Spark

Beijing went completely dark.

No backup power. No transit. No elevator music. Nothing.

At first, cars stopped. Then screens froze and after that, streetlights blinked out.

But something else happened too.

The city paused.

And that's when the shift began.

What People Did Without Power

Neighbors lit candles and shared portable power banks.

Shops opened their doors and offered food before it spoiled.

Families sat on rooftops, watching the stars for the first time in years.

Without screens to scroll, people talked to each other.

They took long walks, wrote in their diaries, and even picked up hobbies like knitting.

And then, they improvised. Restaurants set up solar cookers, a group of teens used bike generators to power charging stations, and parks handed out manual water pumps and gravity-powered lights.

When the grid came back six hours later, analysts discovered something shocking:

In just one blackout, Beijing had saved more energy than it normally would in a full month.

Water consumption dropped by 30%, traffic-related emissions fell to near-zero, and power demand rebounded *lower* than before, because people realized how much they didn't need.

The lights had gone out. And for the first time, people could *see* what was possible.

The Global Ripple

They called it The Six-Hour Spark, and it lit a fire around the world.

In Singapore, Sunday became "Power Pause Day." Families unplugged together and loved it.

In Nairobi, teens engineered wind-powered phone chargers using scrap bike parts and shared them across neighborhoods.

In Oslo, kinetic energy tiles were added to train stations, generating power from footsteps.

Even Times Square dimmed its billboards for an hour each week, a global symbol that progress didn't always need to glow.

And it all started with one... accidental unplugging, thanks to Ellie!

Ellie and I stood on a rooftop, watching Beijing come back online. But now, there were community-powered stations, window gardens, and local energy hubs.

Ellie nudged me. "So, uh... what now?"

The Reminder appeared beside us, now dressed as an electrical engineer.

"You brought the light back," she said. "But more importantly, you helped people remember how to live without it."

A self-driving taxi zipped past below, blaring a weirdly catchy song about battery swapping stations.

Ellie snorted, "okay. I think we just made China... cool?"

I laughed, "let's charge into our next mission."

FIFTEEN

–2040–

THE BANK THAT FIRED EVERYONE

SDG 8: Decent Work and Economic Growth in Switzerland

I landed hard, because, of course, I did.

Cold, polished marble met my face.

Ellie crashed beside me, knocking over a decorative umbrella stand. She laughed, "okay, not my most elegant entrance."

I peeled myself off the floor. We were inside a banking hall straight out of a sci-fi movie. Towering glass buildings appeared sterile and unwelcoming to humans. Holographic stock tickers floated mid-air, flashing words like 'MARGIN CALL' and 'DIGITAL GOLD,' neither of which sounded fun. AI banking assistants glided around, whispering financial advice to people who definitely weren't people.

Then I noticed the problem.

There were no humans, just machines.

Zurich's legendary financial district, once full of bankers in crisp suits, was now run entirely by AI.

No tellers, managers, or analysts...just cold, efficient algorithms running the show.

The Reminder appeared beside us, looking like a disgruntled ex-employee clutching a now useless ID badge. "Human labor became too expensive. They replaced the entire workforce with robots."

Ellie frowned. "So... what? They fired everyone?"

The Reminder nodded bleakly. "TitanCorp's CEO, Silas Corvin, launched Project Profit Prime, a fully automated banking system. No salaries, sick days, or human error...just an economy run by machines."

When we stepped outside, I nearly tripped over a man in a Hugo Boss tie paired with sweatpants and desperation.

The streets were flooded with former bankers, but not in suits. They were unemployed.

Some sold overpriced fondue on fold-out tables, chanting things like, "Buy low, melt high!"

One guy had turned his old briefcase into a grill, flipping grilled cheese with the precision of a hedge fund manager hedging cheddar.

Then, a giant hologram of Silas Corvin flickered to life above a skyscraper.

"Welcome to the future of banking!" Corvin declared, flashing a villainous billionaire grin. "With TitanCorp's automation, our economy is more efficient than ever—no wasteful spending on salaries! No human error! Just pure, beautiful, profit."

I tightened my grip on the edge of the table. "But if nobody has a paycheck, how are they supposed to—"

Corvin kept talking.

"They take out loans."

The Reminder leaned into us with a stern and concerned voice, "if you don't fix this, people will own nothing except debt."

I had seen enough. "Send us back. We're stopping Project Profit Prime before it starts."

And just like that, we were yanked back to 2025.

SIXTEEN

–2025–

WE FOUGHT A SECURITY DRONE WITH CHOCOLATE BARS

SDG 8: Decent Work and Economic Growth in Switzerland

When we opened our eyes, we found ourselves inside a very expensive gala.

There were crystal chandeliers everywhere. Across the room was a string quartet entertaining the rich and hydrated elite of Switzerland, as they sipped their espressos from gold-rimmed cups.

A massive holographic ad flickered above the stage:

TITANCORP PRESENTS: THE FUTURE OF BANKING!

100% AUTOMATED FINANCES. NO HUMANS
NECESSARY. FASTER PROFITS.
MORE GROWTH. LESS... PEOPLE.

Ellie grunted, "I hate that they just said 'less people' like it's a good thing."

The Reminder appeared beside us, looking like a very stressed financial analyst. "This is where it begins. Corvin launches Project Profit Prime, replaces half the workforce, and everything spirals."

I nodded, "then let's crash this party."

We slipped past security, dodging a robotic champagne server (because, of course, they had those), and found TitanCorp's central AI control hub.

Ellie didn't waste any time. "Alright, time to introduce this thing to the joys of system failure."

We hacked TitanCorp's AI assistant. Instead of cold, efficient banking strategies, it now recommended financial advice based on fortune cookies. We tanked Project Profit Prime before it even launched.

Across the room, a wealthy investor frowned at his AI banking assistant. "It says... 'Sometimes the best investment is friendship'?"

Corvin's face turned red. "WHO DID THIS?!"

Escape the Security Drone

We ran.

A security drone whirred to life, flashing red, "INTRUDERS DETECTED."

I skidded to a stop. We were trapped.

Next to me? A Swiss chocolate fountain.

Ellie grabbed the nearest Toblerone like it was Excalibur. "Weapon of choice?"

I snatched another Toblerone, "dual-wielding."

The drone fired. We swung.

WHACK.

Toblerone met robotic steel.

Nothing happened.

Ellie yelled, "okay, so maybe we should've gone with something stronger!"

The drone adjusted its aim.

I panicked and grabbed a bowl of fondue. FLUNG IT.

SPLAT.

The drone short-circuited, sparks flew.

Ellie laughed,"well, I'm never underestimating Swiss chocolate again."

The Cheese Heist

We needed a quick escape.

Ellie ran into the first shop she saw.

It wasn't an exit.

It was a cheese shop.

Ellie frowned, "uh, why do they keep handing me cheese?"

The shopkeeper beamed, "would you like some Emmental? Gruyère?"

I yelled, "Ellie, this isn't an exit! You walked into a cheese shop!"

Then the bank security alarms blared.

Ellie panicked, grabbed a massive wheel of Gruyère, and yelled, "CHEESE SHIELD!"

To be fair... it kind of worked.

We barreled out of the shop, launching cheese wheels behind us like dairy-based grenades.

We didn't stop until we reached the train station. A few hours, two trains, and one melted chocolate bar later, we arrived at Lucerne.

The vibe? Very different. We met a group of twenty-somethings outside a café. They weren't sipping espressos. They were coding, prototyping and arguing about startup pitches and economic justice. Their organization?

"New Swiss Deal."

We helped launch an initiative where young people received government-backed microgrants to launch community businesses—eco-tech, ethical fashion, skill-sharing platforms. Each team had to hire locally, mentor interns, and share profits with employees.

Ellie joined a co-op that designed solar-powered delivery bikes. I helped create a coding bootcamp in a re-purposed watch factory. Old workers taught craftsmanship. Newbies taught them apps. It worked.

Unemployment began to drop. Remote freelancers coexisted with hands-on builders. The economy wasn't just growing, it was pulsing with ideas.

Even better? The Swiss government adopted the "Shared Startup Fund" and exported the model to other nations.

The Reminder appeared beside us, smiling from ear to ear. "Decent work. Decent future."

Then the portal opened up.

SEVENTEEN

– 2 1 2 5 –

THE SMART CITY THAT DIDN'T SEE US COMING

SDG 9: Industry, Innovation, and Infrastructure

I crashed into something hard, cold, and definitely not cutting-edge memory foam.

The air whooshed out of my lungs as I tumbled onto a neon-blue surface, my face smashing through what looked like... a hologram?

Blueprints of futuristic highways, AI-powered train networks, and sleek glass skyscrapers flickered around me. For a second, it felt like I'd fallen through the loading screen of a game that hadn't fully rendered yet.

Ellie, of course, did not stick the landing. She crashed sideways into a pile of VR headsets, setting off a symphony of startup jingles and error beeps. One headset slipped over her eyes and declared,

"Welcome to Zen World: Please find your inner peace."

"Okay," she grumbled. "I take back what I said earlier. I miss the wastelands. At least they had soft dirt."

I pushed myself up and looked around. We were in Bengaluru, India's tech capital.

This was the heart of India's innovation boom.

The place where dreams of the future were supposed to be built.

And yet...

Instead of the bustling city of progress I expected, I found something oddly silent. Hovering billboards flickered, as thousands of drones zipped through the air delivering chai, weaving between self-driving cars. Glass skyscrapers stretched toward the sky, their LED panels looping endless promo videos of "The City of Tomorrow."

However, underneath the glow, the cracks were already forming.

The iconic MG Road, once alive with endless honking and street vendors shouting about the best masala dosa, was eerily quiet. There were no traffic jams or rickshaws squeezing into impossible spaces. Instead, there was just a half-finished monorail station covered in dust.

The famous Vidhana Soudha building stood in the distance but entire wings were abandoned, left half-built when funding ran dry.

Over at Electronic City, the hub of India's biggest tech companies, entire office towers stood empty, their windows dark. The places where some of the greatest software engineers in the world once worked? Now glorified ghost towns.

Even the Bengaluru Palace, which had stood for over a century, had cracks running through its walls.

Ellie took a deep breath, taking it all in. "Wow, the Silicon Valley of India sure looks... abandoned."

The Reminder stood next to us, now looking like a tech startup CEO in a hoodie.

He gestured toward the glitching skyline. "Welcome to Bengaluru's future. Well... what's left of it."

The Reminder paused to take a sip of his kombucha and then continued, "turns out," he said, "when we build with people at the heart of it instead of just for profit, communities actually thrive."

Ellie poked at a holographic blueprint of a futuristic bridge. It glitched violently, half-disappearing before flickering back into existence.

"So, uh..." she said. "Doesn't look like this lasted long."

I tightened my jaw. "We're fixing this."

Ellie sighed, pulling herself out of the VR headset graveyard.

"Yeah, yeah, of course we are. But, uh, how exactly?"

I was determined, "we go back. We change the way this city is built before it turns into this mess."

Before Ellie could argue, the flash of light surrounded us.

And the next thing I knew—

We were falling again.

EIGHTEEN

–2025–

WE BROKE THE WIFI
OF THE FUTURE

SDG 9: Industry, Innovation, and Infrastructure

We suddenly appeared smack in the middle of a 2025 tech expo, right where it all started.

Sure, it looked like progress. There were massive AI-generated city plans floating above us, drones delivered steaming cups of chai to investors, and self-driving electric rickshaws hummed past on their designated smart lanes.

But the problems were surfacing, just hidden under all the neon and buzzwords.

I barely had time to take it all in before someone handed me a tablet and said, "you're up next."

I stuttered, "I-I'm what now?"

"Presenting the WiFi initiative," the guy said, already walking off. "Make sure the system goes live smoothly."

I turned to Ellie, "okay, I have no idea what I just agreed to, but let's roll with it."

A timer counted down on a giant holographic screen: 5... 4... 3...

All we had to do was activate Bengaluru's first city-wide high-speed WiFi system. No big deal.

2... 1...

An AI voice boomed overhead.

"Critical system overload. Rebooting Bengaluru in 3... 2... 1..."

The entire city lost internet access.

For a second, there was dead silence.

Then—absolute chaos.

A chai drone spiraled out of control, slamming into a robotic samosa cart. Investors screamed as their portfolios vanished into the digital void. Somewhere, someone yelled in Kannada, which I was pretty sure translated to "you destroyed my stock market!"

Ellie gasped, "did we just... unplug all of Bengaluru?"

I winced, "uh, maybe?"

I had no idea what we were doing, but I'd watched enough heist movies to know that if you look like you're supposed to be somewhere, people don't question you.

So we ran.

We ducked into the control room and got to work: Frantic rewiring, emergency system resets, some light bribery in the form of free coffee.

Finally, after an endless amount of button-mashing, emergency system resets, and one very close call with an overheating server, we got the WiFi back online.

Not just back online but better.

Turns out, the system wasn't just glitchy, it was designed to favor corporate networks and luxury neighborhoods. Meaning, if you were in a high-rise investment firm, you had lightning-fast WiFi. But if you were a student in a rural village? You were still waiting for your one Wikipedia page to load... from 2015.

So we rewired the entire access grid. Across Bengaluru, the changes hit fast, like chai cooling down way too quickly. Free, high-speed WiFi spread across the city. Suddenly, nobody had to huddle outside cafés for a signal. Factory workers weren't just stuck with outdated manuals. They could actually watch training videos instead of relying on that one guy who "swore he knew how to fix it." Students in remote villages logged into virtual classrooms for the first time, which was great because education shouldn't depend on whether you live near a decent school.

Bengaluru wasn't just connected, it was leveling up.

Bengaluru didn't just survive, it thrived. Factories ran on clean energy, high-speed electric trains connected cities, while AI-powered farms grew food sustainably and students in the most remote villages accessed world-class education.

Ellie was full of excitement. "So... do we finally get those flying cars Bollywood keeps promising?!"

I sighed, "one problem at a time."

The Reminder, now looking like an engineer testing a solar-powered drone, smiled.

"You did good."

I exhaled, watching the once-crumbling roads now lined with electric buses, self-driving taxis, and actual bike lanes.

India wasn't just keeping up with the future, it *was* the future.

We felt ourselves being pulled forward.

On to our next mission.

NINETEEN

–2030–

THE INVISIBLE LINE

SDG 10: Reduced Inequalities

I didn't expect to land in a helicopter!

But there I was—strapped into a seat beside Ellie, headset crackling in my ears, the rotors thundering overhead as the helicopter tilted hard to the right. Sydney unfolded beneath us like a postcard.

"OH MY GOSH, WE'RE IN A HELICOPTER!" Ellie shrieked, grabbing the sides of her seat like it was going to fly off without her.

The Reminder, dressed like an elite rescue pilot, aviators, bomber jacket, the works, barely glanced back. "Welcome aboard."

"Where are we going?" I asked, trying to sound calm, like I wasn't one unexpected gust away from screaming.

"To where the story splits," she said.

Ellie leaned forward, pressing her face to the window. "From up here? Everything looks... amazing."

And she was right. The sun glinted off the Harbour Bridge. Yachts glittered like polished shells in the bay. Downtown buzzed with holographic billboards showing ads for "hyper-luxury wellness towers" and "AI butler packages."

"Watch this," The Reminder said.

The chopper banked left, gliding over the Parramatta River. Everything changed.

The glitter stopped.

Roads gave way to potholes. Parks turned into overgrown lots. The buildings? Abandoned with broken windows. Rusted machinery sat in factory yards. Playgrounds were empty. It was like someone had drawn a line and said, *Here, progress. There, leftovers.*

"Wait," Ellie muttered. "This is still Sydney."

"Technically," The Reminder said. "But no one ever bothered to build the schools, businesses or public transportation on the other side.

Ellie leaned out her side of the chopper, watching the rows of neglected buildings slip by beneath us. "So, we need to bring the schools, businesses and public transportation there too."

The Reminder smiled. "That's the key, reducing inequalities."

TWENTY

−2025−

BRIDGING A CITY

SDG 11: Reduced Inequalities

I found myself in the middle seat of a Sydney bus.

It was a *very* full, *very* hot Sydney bus…but at least softer than my usual hard landings.

Ellie got the window seat beside me and was fanning herself with a crumpled flyer.

A toddler wailed. Someone's elbow jabbed my ribs. My leg stuck to the vinyl seat like it had been glued there in a heatwave.

But this wasn't just any bus.

We were on the west side of the Parramatta River, the part of the city *not* featured in the tourism ads. The bus crawled past boarded-up shops, faded murals, and school buildings that looked like they'd been donated by the 1980s and then immediately forgotten.

I leaned over to talk to the woman sitting beside me, her arms full of groceries and a half-finished crochet sweater.

"How far are you going?"

"Two hours," she said with a tired smile. "Work's across the bridge. Closest job I could find."

"And the school?" Ellie asked, looking over at the boy sitting beside the woman.

She sighed. "Three teachers quit this year. My son hasn't had a proper science class in months. They say it's hard to get teachers to stay."

The guy in front of us, wearing a grease-stained work shirt, turned around.

"Doesn't matter if you study or not," he said. "There's no jobs over here anyway. Businesses don't set up shop on this side of the river. No customers, no foot traffic, no money."

On the other side of the Parramatta River, Sydney was a solar-powered, glass-walled marvel with electric ferries and AI-powered classrooms. Over here? It was a daily marathon just to show up.

That's when the idea started forming.

We hopped off the bus at the end of the line and looked around. This part of town didn't even have a proper transit hub.

"What if we don't wait for business and education to come to this side?" I said. "What if we bring it here?"

Ellie looked puzzled. "Like what? Teleportation?"

"Better," I said, grinning. "Pop-ups."

Operation Bridge the City

Step one: Mobile Opportunity Units.

We partnered with a few surprisingly enthusiastic city council members and set up converted buses as mobile career centers, Wi-Fi hotspots, and tutoring stations. These weren't just resources, they were *bridges*. Each one brought jobs, classes, or business mentors straight into neighborhoods that had been left off the city's investment maps.

Step two: Transit for All.

We worked with urban planners to expand bus routes and introduce "Bridge Cards"—free rides for job-seekers, students, and teachers crossing into the city center.

Step three: Flip the Tour.

Remember how we toured the under-resourced neighborhoods with city leaders? This time, we did the reverse. We brought students from the forgotten schools into the heart of Sydney's financial district—VR labs, robotics firms, creative agencies, so they could *see* what was possible.

On the forgotten side of the river, pop-up markets opened in the old bus depot. A startup incubator was set up in an abandoned warehouse. One school got so much community support, they added a greenhouse and student-run coffee cart.

Ellie and I stood at the bridge, watching it all.

"This," she said, "feels like a real connection."

I added, "and it started with a hot bus and a conversation."

The Reminder, standing nearby with a transit map and iced tea, smiled.

"You didn't just shorten the distance," she said. "You made both sides visible."

Then the bright light surrounded us again.

New place. New mission.

TWENTY-ONE

-2200-

THE AMAZON IS GONE

SDG 11: Sustainable Cities and Communities

L et's just say: visiting the Amazon Rainforest used to sound cool...except when there's no rainforest left.

I hit the ground and rolled through what I first thought was sand. But sand doesn't crinkle like discarded chip bags. I sat up and realized I'd landed in a sea of plastic; bottles, wrappers, netting, broken drones, half a sandal, like the entire planet had dumped its trash into Brazil's lungs.

Ellie landed a few feet away, brushing sticky, sun-baked film from her jacket. "This is... the Amazon?"

I stared at the cracked, barren earth beneath us. "Used to be."

Gone were the towering trees, no canopy, no vines, no birds or monkeys...just heat and the constant crackle of dry, poisoned soil. Every breath felt like inhaling a sunburn.

We climbed a small hill, well, more of a plastic mound, and

got our first look at the ocean.

To our left, the coastline, or what used to be the coastline. The ocean was a soup of plastics. We couldn't even see the waves because they were covered with Styrofoam, tangled fishing lines, and glittery party trash that never got cleaned up after Carnival.

The Reminder stepped up beside us, wearing a scorched neon-orange safety vest over a dirt-streaked city engineer's uniform. "They expanded into the rainforest, cut down trees for concrete, bulldozed habitats for high-rises and highways, and ultimately disrupted the ecosystem."

He gestured toward the coastline in the distance, where the water looked a sickly gray.

"And the plastic? It didn't just ruin the oceans, it poisoned the rivers that fed the forest. Roots choked, animals vanished, and even the rain changed."

Ellie crouched beside a crumbling tree stump, brushing ash off its surface. "They built over nature without thinking what the consequences would be."

The Reminder nodded sadly. "Ellie kicked a crushed soda can. "Why didn't they just stop?"

"They didn't think they needed to," he said. "They thought it was someone else's job."

I could feel the portal pulling us in, "I guess it's our job now."

TWENTY-TWO

–2025–

CARNIVAL CHAOS

SDG 11: Sustainable Cities and Communities

I clung to the side of Ellie's runaway float, my heart pounding like a samba drum in my chest. The float, a giant, glittering jaguar made of rainforests and sparkles, swerved down Rio's crowded avenue, nearly flattening a street vendor and a guy trying to sell plastic toucan figurines. I didn't know if I was more terrified of the float or the fact that Ellie was perched on top, waving a samba baton like she was about to conduct an orchestra of chaos.

"This is *not* how I planned to save the rainforest!" I yelled, ducking under a flailing papier-mâché paw that looked like it had been inspired by a nightmare.

A few hours ago, we had seen the future of Rio, where favelas sprawled over the jungle and smog choked the streets. Now, a bulldozer was clearing land in the middle of the parade route, completely ignoring the fact that, oh I don't know, *we were on a float trying to save the city's future?!*

"Ellie, get me closer to that bulldozer!" I shouted, as the float lurched again, nearly throwing me off. I swear, it had a mind of its own. Ellie looked at me like I'd just sprouted wings, but somehow, she managed to steer the jaguar in a wild arc. I'm not sure how—maybe she accidentally hit the right lever, or maybe the universe was just *that* weird.

With a dramatic screech, our float smacked into the bulldozer, causing it to grind to a halt. I leapt off the float and scrambled onto the bulldozer's hood, striking a pose I thought was very "action hero meets environmental activist."

"PEOPLE OF RIO!" I shouted, in my best dramatic voice. "The rainforest has had enough!" The crowd didn't seem to mind, especially when a drumbeat started up like a soundtrack to my perfect moment of eco-heroism. "No more bulldozing! We need to protect what's left!"

Ellie jumped up beside me, holding a flaming samba baton like it was no big deal. "From now on," she yelled, "let's expand *upwards*! Rooftop gardens, vertical housing!" She jabbed the baton skyward. "The jungle doesn't need to be sacrificed for urban sprawl!"

People cheered us on, like maybe we weren't just two crazy kids on a float in the middle of a parade. I spotted a few architects exchanging thumbs-up and offering ideas about turning empty spaces into vertical forests. It was like a revolution was taking root, one samba step at a time.

And then... *plastic.* Everywhere. Cups, confetti, food wrappers—an explosion of waste swirling around us like a tornado of trash. I could feel my stomach sink. We were barely making progress on saving the rainforest, and now we had to deal with Rio's other big issue.

Ellie nearly slipped on a banana peel (ironically, it was biodegradable, but still). "Plan Clean Sweep?" she asked, face smeared with glitter and confusion.

I agreed. "You bet. Let's do it."

We cupped our hands and started yelling over the music, "RECYCLING CHALLENGE! Competition starting NOW!" I said, trying to sound like a coach at the championship game. Ellie added, "FREE churrasco for a year for whoever picks up the most trash!" which was totally unapproved, but who cared? We were saving Rio.

At first, no one cared. Most of the crowd was still dancing, oblivious to the mountain of garbage collecting at their feet. But Ellie, ever the resourceful one, grabbed a samba school's flag and clambered onto a bench. "Unidos da Limpeza!" she shouted, like she'd invented an entire samba school in thirty seconds. "Let's clean up this mess!"

People actually listened. Dancers joined in. A kid in a mini Neymar costume sprinted past, clutching an empty confetti popper to deposit at one of the new "Confetti Bottle Deposit" kiosks the city had set up this year. They gave out Carnival tokens in exchange for the plastic waste. It was working. And it was working fast.

Before long, Rio was looking like an environmentally conscious carnival. The deposit-return system was a hit, the streets were cleaner, and even a few toucans seemed to join the celebration, flying overhead like a good omen.

I planted the sapling someone had handed me earlier, in a little patch of soil near the curb. "For the future," a glittery-dressed grandmother told me as she passed by, giving me a thumbs-up.

Ellie and I leaned against the jaguar float, catching our breath. "Well," she said, brushing glitter off her arms, "I guess we did it."

I laughed. "Did we? We stopped a bulldozer, got Rio to recycle, and turned Carnival into a green revolution in *two hours*. What's next?"

Just then, The Reminder appeared next to us, sipping something fruity out of a coconut. "Nice work," she said, like we hadn't just transformed an entire city with a samba parade. "But you're not done yet."

I sighed. "Figures."

Ellie yawned, rubbing her eyes. "Can we at least nap between disasters?"

The shimmering portal reappeared in front of us, glowing gold and green, and a very grumpy-looking dolphin wearing a Carnival hat swam through it. It gave us an unimpressed look.

I rolled my eyes. "No rest for the sustainable."

And just like that, we were off again.

TWENTY-THREE

– 2 1 2 5 –

MORE! BIGGER! FASTER! ...WORSE!

SDG 12: Responsible Consumption and Production

I was covered by a pile of jeans. Thousands of them; blue, black, acid-washed, ripped, high-rise, low-rise, and whatever-rise came out in 2087. Many still had the price tags.

Ellie pulled a rhinestone jacket off her face. "Okay... who turned Madrid into a clearance bin?"

I stood up, knee-deep in a sea of abandoned clothes. It stretched in every direction like some forgotten textile ocean. Torn shirts flapped in the wind. Dresses hung from collapsed buildings like haunted flags. A billboard half-buried in shredded fabric read:

"NEW DROP! NEXT DROP! ALWAYS DROP!"

The air reeked of chemicals—dyes, synthetic fibers, and, weirdly, burnt faux leather.

"This place looks like a mall exploded," Ellie said.

The Reminder appeared beside us in a faded fluorescent vest that read, "Responsible Consumption/Production," holding a broken hanger like it was a crime scene clue.

"They called it fast fashion," he said, picking his way through the mounds. "Turns out, the faster it was made, the faster it destroyed everything."

We wandered toward what used to be the Manzanares River. Now? A trench filled with shredded cotton, microplastic soup, and enough discarded festival wristbands to host a rave for the next century. Factories once powered by dirty energy loomed overhead, now silent and collapsed under their own waste.

"Fashion flipped faster than common sense," I mumbled.

We stood for a moment, surrounded by silent towers of trend-trash, the skyline practically stitched together with yesterday's outfits.

"Alright," I said. "Let's change the story."

The shimmer lit up around us—soft this time, like fabric in a breeze.

And just like that, we were gone.

Time to give Madrid a makeover that actually mattered.

TWENTY-FOUR

–2025–

WHEN LESS IS MORE

SDG 12: Responsible Consumption and Production

W e found ourselves climbing out of a mountain of sweaters.

Literally.

I popped my head out of the itchy avalanche, coughing up a fuzzball. "Okay. Not lava, not garbage—progress."

Ellie emerged next to me, holding up a neon-orange turtle-neck. "Why does this exist?"

We were in the backroom of a massive department store in Madrid. Shelves towered with unsold clothes. There were liter-ally thousands of winter jackets, snow boots, and wool scarves... in August. It was like a fashion apocalypse bunker.

We slipped past racks of rejected trends and found a bored employee scanning barcodes on a tablet.

"Hey," I said, "what happens to all this stuff?"

He shrugged. "We box it, toss it on a truck, and it gets dumped outside the city."

Ellie's jaws dropped.

I turned to her. "We're following that truck."

And that's how we ended up sprinting through the store's underground lot and jumping into the back of a delivery truck labeled *Logística Urgente*.

Except...

Ten minutes later, we realized we had not boarded the merchandise truck.

We were sitting between two very large, very unimpressed bulls.

Ellie slowly turned to me. "Leyth..."

"I know."

"This is not the recycling facility."

"I *know*."

The truck lurched and stopped. We peeked out the back.

A bullring...an actual bullfight. It was chaotic with people running to take their seats while trumpets were blaring.

"Oh, great," Ellie said under her breath. "You're about to be mistaken for the opening act."

A man in a velvet jacket pointed at me. "¡Ahí está el nuevo torero!"

Ellie snorted. "Here's our new Matador!"

I stumbled into the ring wearing a fashion poncho, holding a piece of red fabric I'd yanked off a clearance rack. The bull pawed the dirt. The crowd cheered.

"OKAY," I shouted. "Let's not do this!"

The bull charged.

I threw the poncho.

It hit a hot dog vendor.

Chaos erupted.

Ellie, meanwhile, had slipped into the announcer booth and hit the emergency evacuation button. Turns out, Spanish bullrings *do* have one.

The crowd panicked, the bulls got distracted by popcorn, and I dive-rolled into a pile of hay.

A moment later, we were back outside the arena, out of breath and definitely off the wrong truck.

"You good?" Ellie asked.

"I may never eat beef again."

Eventually, we did find the right truck.

We followed it to the dumping site. There were hills of never-worn clothes, some still with tags. It hit us hard.

So we called every manufacturer and retailer who would listen and pitched a system.

A global tracker: Retailers would scan leftover stock, upload the data, and manufacturers could adjust future production. No more over-ordering, no more five identical jackets in six sizes.

Leftover items? Automatically rerouted to countries that needed clothing: refugee camps, disaster zones, remote villages.

We teamed up with NGOs, coders, and a few surprisingly helpful fashion interns. The Circular Supply Initiative was born.

And slowly, Madrid stopped being a city of waste.

We left the warehouse that day surrounded by reused fabrics, recycled sneakers, and, thankfully, no bulls.

The Reminder appeared beside us, sipping a fruity Brazilian juice from a compostable cup.

"You two really know how to stir things up," she said.

Ellie giggled. "We prefer our chaos with flair."

"And no horns," I added.

The shimmer glowed around us, ready to pull us into whatever mess was next.

But this time? We weren't just fixing problems.

We were redesigning the system.

With style.

TWENTY-FIVE

–2165–

WELCOME TO SMOGPOCALYPSE

SDG 13: Climate Action

I appeared next to Ellie inside a moving car, which then proceeded to swerve violently and nearly sideswipe a flaming food delivery drone.

"WHY ARE WE IN A MOVING VEHICLE?!" I shouted.

"Because," came a familiar voice from the front seat, "you needed to see this."

The Reminder was in the driver's seat, calmly gripping the wheel in a hazmat suit that looked like it had survived both a fire and a fashion disaster. A cracked oxygen mask covered her face. "Seatbelts, please," she added cheerfully, "unless you want to fly out the windshield in the next traffic burst."

Ellie and I sat up at the same time, and that's when it hit me. The air.

I gagged and yanked on the emergency oxygen mask hanging from the car ceiling like it was an airplane from Doom Airlines. Ellie already had hers on and was eyeing the outside world like it might lunge through the window and attack us.

"Okay," she wheezed. "So...what apocalyptic nightmare are we in today?"

I looked out the window. We were in Singapore, stuck in bumper-to-bumper traffic along the Pan Island Expressway. There were hundreds of cars, some futuristic, some ancient, all of them idling, honking, and coughing out fumes like they were trying to beat each other in a "Who Can Destroy the Atmosphere Faster?" competition.

Pedestrians walked along the roads in full-body UV suits. Some wore oxygen tanks on their backs. Above us, the outline of Marine Bay Sands was just barely visible. The sky was a foggy gray.

Ellie whispered, "Where's the sun?"

The Reminder turned the wheel and pulled into the slowest-moving lane I've ever seen in my life. "Still there," she said solemnly. "Just more lethal now with the pierced ozone layer and UV rays coming through like lasers. You'll notice the fashionable silver umbrellas everyone's carrying—those are radiation shields."

Ellie shook her head. "I don't see any green parks or even a blue sky, just traffic and more traffic. It's like the Earth got paved over with fumes."

"We'll fix it," I said, my voice muffled behind my mask. "We have to."

The Reminder glanced in the rearview mirror, her eyes fierce.

"Then buckle up," she said. "Because reversing climate collapse starts with slamming the brakes."

And just like that, the portal opened up, right in the middle of the gridlock.

We were heading back to 2025, to stop the smog before it swallowed the city whole.

TWENTY-SIX

−2025−

IT STARTED WITH ONE BUS

SDG 13: Climate Action

Remind me again," Ellie whispered, "why we're breaking into a bus depot at 3 a.m. with a croissant and a hairpin?"

"Because," I said, wedging the hairpin into the rusted lock, "we're about to save Singapore from becoming a human-sized toaster oven. And also, we need to eat something."

With a dramatic *click*, the lock gave way, and the gate creaked open like it had a bad back.

Inside, rows of dusty city buses sat in the dark like retired guardians of a time when people actually took public transport. Most were covered in cobwebs. One had a bird's nest in the side mirror.

Ellie peeked through a window. "These things used to run all over the city, right? What happened?"

"They got replaced," said a voice behind us.

We spun around.

The Reminder was there, leaning casually on a bench, dressed like a retired bus driver in khaki shorts and a faded SBS Transit cap. His name tag read, "Mr. Enough-Driving-Alone." He took a sip from a metal kopi cup and looked at the buses.

"Everyone wanted their own car," he said. "Even when the air turned toxic and the roads stopped moving, no one wanted to give them up."

The Reminder tossed me a key. "Start with the oldest one. People need a reminder."

We climbed into the first bus in the row. Ellie jabbed a button at random. The wipers squeaked to life. "You sure you know how to drive this?"

"Totally," I said, fiddling under the dash. "As long as it's like Mario Kart but with brakes."

Finally—*VROOOOOOOOOOOOM*—the engine rumbled awake.

We burst out of the depot and straight into downtown traffic, narrowly avoiding a hawker cart.

People stared. This bus hadn't run in years, and suddenly it was barreling down Robinson Road with "NOT IN SERVICE" flashing like a challenge.

I tapped the screen. "Let's change that."

Our first passengers? Two makciks (aunties) with groceries and a sleepy construction worker who'd been waiting forty-five minutes for a bus that never came.

"This is free?" the guy asked.

"Yep," I said. "Just tell your friends."

By the time we hit Marina Bay, the Carbon Buster was standing-room only.

We posted photos. Shared videos. Started a hashtag: #TakeTheBusLah

Overnight, people remembered what buses could do. They were faster, cheaper, and way less likely to cause an asthma attack.

The Green Reboot

Bus companies called us. So did city planners. So did, weirdly, a K-pop fan account that wanted to name a bus after us. Within weeks:

- Rusty buses were electrified.
- New bus lanes were added.
- An app launched to track buses in real time—with built-in air quality data.
- Offices gave bonuses to employees who used ride shares or public transit.
- Carpool networks expanded, giving perks like carpool-only lanes.

Ellie pointed to the news on her phone. "Taxi unions are partnering with Mass Rapid Transit now to offer shared routes and discounted rides."

Buses weren't boring anymore. They were the cool option equipped with air-conditioning and WiFi-capability.

People ditched solo drives for smart rides. Moms organized school runs together. Teens used the new GreenRide app to find the fastest carpool to campus. Even uncles at kopi shops bragged about how little they'd spent on fuel that month.

I stood in a packed hawker center, watching people tap on the app we helped launch.

The Reminder, now sipping a sugarcane juice in the shade. "You made movement mean something again."

Ellie leaned against the bus stop, arms crossed. "Feels good."

She glanced up at the sky, still bright, but not the lung-melting yellow it used to be. "The air even smells... normal."

"For now," the Reminder said, as the shimmer began forming around us again.

Ellie complained, "no nap?"

"No nap," I said. "We're on a roll."

Next stop: who knows. But we're not braking anytime soon.

TWENTY-SEVEN

–2170–

THE SEA OF NIGHTMARES

SDG 14: Life Below Water

W e landed with a dull *thunk*, not on land, not on sand, but inside a submarine.

I looked up, disoriented. Ellie was upside down in a harness seat beside me, staring like someone who'd just been rudely shaken out of a dream and dropped into a nightmare.

Outside the thick glass windows, it was pitch black, until the sub's lights flickered on.

And then we saw it.

The sea wasn't blue. It wasn't even murky green.

It was dark, dreary, and lifeless.

We pressed closer to the window.

Fish, if you could even call them that, floated past with bulging eyes and translucent skin stretched thin over distorted bones. One had a plastic bottle lodged in its torso like it had grown around it. Another slithered by, its tail fused with aluminum, like it had inherited a soda can as a body part. Jellyfish drifted past, their tentacles tangled in shopping bags. A crab crawled along the seafloor dragging what looked like the lid of a peanut butter jar as a shell.

Ellie whispered, "what happened to them?"

The Reminder, appearing in the pilot seat wearing a deep-sea diving suit patched together with old fishing net, didn't look away from the controls.

"They adapted," she said quietly. "To our garbage, chemicals, and neglect."

We drifted past the ruins of a coral reef, except there was no color left. The coral was bleached and brittle, snapped in half like burnt toast. Plastic straws stuck out of it like needles. Broken flip-flops and fishing wire weaved through the branches like parasites.

Out in the distance, something darker loomed.

A shape moved, huge, slow, and glinting. For a second, I thought it was a whale, but as it turned, I saw it wasn't normal!

It had fins made of torn tarp. Its barnacled body was studded with bottle caps. Its head? A crushed detergent container.

It stared straight at us with one foggy eye, then disappeared into the smoggy deep.

Ellie took a step back, pale. "We did that?"

The Reminder responded, "the sea didn't just die. We reprogrammed it with everything we threw away."

I looked at the twisted remains of Poseidon's kingdom and felt a deep, burning shame. This was Greece, a place where gods once ruled the waves. Now, it was an underwater graveyard for everything we never thought we'd have to face again.

Ellie's voice was quiet. "We've got to fix this."

And just as the submarine creaked from the pressure, the shimmer formed around us again.

This time, I didn't hesitate.

We weren't swimming away from the mess.

We were going back to stop it from ever happening.

TWENTY-EIGHT

– 2025 –

I CAME, I SWAM, I CLEANED THE OCEAN

SDG 14: Life Below Water

When the shimmer spat us out again, I braced for impact—another pile of fish guts, maybe a mutant jelly-squid surprise.

Instead, I landed in a chair.

A *chair*...with an actual *cushion*.

Ellie plopped down beside me into something squishy that sighed like a beanbag. She whispered, "okay, this can't be right. Did we just get a gentle landing?"

I patted the cushion beneath me like it might vanish. "Either the portal's glitching... or the universe is finally cutting us some slack."

That's when the Reminder appeared, looking disturbingly relaxed in aviators, holding a frosted glass of a Greek lemony drink, probably something called "soumada."

He took a slow sip, then said, "the Earth's finding its balance again. And when the planet breathes easier, so do you."

Ellie raised an eyebrow. "So... the comfier the landing, the healthier the Earth?"

"Roughly," he said, adjusting his shades. "Let's just say equilibrium has perks."

I stretched my legs, still half-convinced I was dreaming. "At this rate, we're two missions away from landing in a hot tub."

The Reminder cracked a smile. "Earn it first."

Step One: Turn Trash into Treasure

Our first stop? A windswept fishing village on Naxos, where we met a gang of feisty *yiayiás*—Greek grandmothers with sharper instincts than Google Maps and zero tolerance for nonsense.

"Χρυσό μου, why waste good net?" one suggested, handing Ellie a basket woven from a cleaned-up ghost net. "Make bags, hats, and money!"

Within days, the docks were buzzing. Old fishing nets were being cleaned, repurposed, and woven into designer accessories. Tourists snapped them up like souvenirs. Fashion houses called it "eco-chic." The Reminder raised his glass. "From pollutant... to profit."

Step Two: Give the Sea a Voice

We needed the Mediterranean to go viral.

So we teamed up with the real influencers, Greece's marine biologists-turned-TikTok legends. They danced with dolphins, broke down ocean acidification in 30 seconds or less, and trained an octopus named Aristotle to pick trash out of the sea.

Ellie joked, "that mollusk is literally smarter than half the kids in my chemistry class."

Step Three: Regrow the Sea

We got government grants to build artificial reefs using ancient Greek shipwreck replicas (because, obviously, Greece has *style*). We teamed up with divers, students, and volunteers to plant coral fragments and restock fish populations sustainably.

Ellie high-fived a scuba diver. "Rebuilding the sea *and* giving Poseidon some ancient street cred? We're unstoppable."

The Reminder watched schools of fish dart through the waters where trash had once floated.

"The ocean remembers," he said. "And forgives if you give it a reason to."

We stood on a sun-warmed dock as the real Santorini sun dipped into an actually blue sea. Clean boats floated nearby. A dolphin splashed beside the pier—not mutant, not glowing, just... free.

Ellie took a deep breath. "Smells like... not death."

I smiled. "Smells like progress."

The shimmer sparkled above us.

And for once, it didn't feel like an escape.

It felt like we'd earned the ride.

TWENTY-NINE

-2180-

THE MUTANT WILDS

SDG 15: Life on Land

I woke up in a cot! A cot with an actual pillow which would've been great if it weren't already occupied...by a lion.

At first, I thought it was a blanket. Then the blanket growled.

I froze. The lion shifted under me with a low, sickly snarl like a motorcycle trying to start underwater.

The Reminder was already standing at the tent's flap, dressed like a safari guide in a dusty khaki shirt and a sun-scorched straw hat, casually sipping something herbal out of a dented tin mug.

"See?" she said, not even flinching. "Told you your landings would get softer. The Earth's healing. Sort of."

Behind her, a real Kenyan ranger scanned the horizon through binoculars.

I scrambled off the lion before it could make me its emotional support snack.

The lion, if you could still call it that, unfolded itself from the dirt.

Its mane was thin and patchy, its skin clung to its bones like forgotten laundry, and one of its eyes glowed a sickly green. It didn't roar so much as wheeze like a haunted accordion.

Ellie landed outside the tent a second later and came face-to-face with something worse.

"What is *that*?" she squeaked.

It was... a wolf? Sort of.

Its legs were too long, its back crooked like it had been glued together wrong, and its mouth was filled with way too many jagged teeth. It snarled, sounding like a blender full of rocks.

The Reminder took a long sip of whatever nightmare tea she was drinking.

"Oh, right," she said. "I forgot to mention, when you destroy ecosystems, the animals don't just vanish. Sometimes... they mutate."

From the woods, more horrors stumbled forward–a giraffe with a neck that barely held its own weight; an elephant missing its tusks, its skin scarred with deep chemical burns; a vulture with half its feathers gone; a hawk with *two heads* and zero chill screeched from a crumbling branch.

Ellie clutched my arm. "Leyth, please tell me we are NOT about to get eaten by radioactive zombie animals."

I swallowed. "I really wish I could."

The Reminder turned grim. "This used to be the Maasai Mara, one of the most biodiverse places on Earth. But we hunted, logged, mined, and paved until there was nothing left. Then nature adapted to our destruction."

I looked around at the cracked, brittle land, at the skeletal trees and poisoned sky.

"Can we fix it?" I asked.

She set down her mug. "Only if you start now."

Ellie took a deep breath. "Okay. Step one—don't get eaten."

"Step two," I added. "save the last living giraffe before it becomes a cryptid."

The shimmer had come, which meant we had work to do.

And judging by the way the lion was eyeballing me again?

We better start fast!

THIRTY

-2025-

THE GREAT REWILDING

SDG 15: Life on Land

The shimmer spat us out right onto a patch of sunbaked Kenyan dirt.

Not a skyscraper in sight, no traffic noise, and definitely no mutant hyenas. Just the golden warmth of the real Maasai Mara—the 2025 version. And this time?

I landed on a camping mat.

With actual padding.

Ellie plopped beside me onto another mat, staring up at the sky. "Okay, either the shimmer's in a good mood, or the Earth's vibe is getting better."

The Reminder, now wearing the same ranger outfit minus the doomsday energy, sipped from a thermos. "Told you. When nature heals, so do your landings."

I took a deep breath. The air smelled like sun and grass,

not burning fur and ecological guilt. "Right," I said, standing. "Let's make sure the future doesn't include a two-headed hawk apocalypse."

Reverse the Damage (With Science and Sweat)

We launched the #RewildTheMara campaign, where schools, tourists, and volunteers signed up to help replant native trees, clean up dumped waste, and build wildlife-safe watering holes.

Even better? We introduced drone-dispersed seed pods that scattered native plants across scorched zones like eco-glitter bombs.

One day, Ellie rode on the back of a seed drone yelling, "FOR NATURE!" like she was in "Avengers: Reforestation Edition."

Bring Back the Rangers

We secured funding to hire and train more wildlife rangers from local communities; people who actually knew the land, loved it, and weren't afraid to chase poachers down on motorcycles.

We even got smart collars installed on at-risk animals to track their movement and protect them from danger.

"Oh cool," Ellie said, watching a rhino's movement on her tablet. "It's like Find My Rhino."

Give Animals Room to Roam

We helped launch a cross-border wildlife corridor program with Kenya, Tanzania, and Uganda. Animals don't care about maps, so we made sure they didn't have to.

Governments signed on. Barriers came down. Migration routes reopened.

And the best part? The animals came back. Real ones, and not the bizarre, mutant type.

Ellie pointed as a herd of elephants marched across the plains. "I swear, that one just winked at me."

Make Conservation Worth It

We created new jobs: park guides, biodiversity tech monitors, wildlife photographers, eco-tourism hosts, rangers. The local economy grew because the land stayed wild, not in spite of it.

We also built *Green Zones*, solar-powered villages that traded in conservation credits and hosted visiting schools from around the world.

"Nature's not just for saving," the Reminder said. "It's for living with."

One Last Look

Back at camp, I watched the sun set behind an acacia tree as giraffes moved across the horizon like living brushstrokes.

No sagging necks. No infected wounds. Just... life.

Ellie stretched out on her mat. "This might be the first time we've actually saved something without being chased by mutant warthogs."

I smiled. "Don't jinx it."

The Reminder, polishing binoculars, grinned. "You've rewilded the land. Let's hope the next place is just as lucky."

The shimmer sparked around us.

And as it pulled us away, I looked back at the Mara, wild and whole again, and thought:

Let's keep Earth interesting, but in a good way.

THIRTY-ONE

$-2160-$

THE WIG, THE GAVEL, AND THE UTTER NONSENSE

SDG 16: Peace, Justice, and Strong Institutions

We suddenly found ourselves in what I *thought* was a parade.

Brass band, glitter, a woman dressed as a giant custard cream twirling down the street.

Then I turned my head... and watched a man in a three-piece suit get arrested for putting milk in before the tea.

Ellie sat up on the pavement beside me. "Okay, softest landing yet. Where are we? The Great British Bake-Off... meets court?"

We were in London... well, sort of. But not the London I knew. There were no Big Ben and double-decker buses. This was a legal circus. Because apparently... the courtroom was now a mobile float.

117

"CASE #3849! Reginald Featherstone—guilty of sneezing during the national anthem. Sentence: thirty days of apologising to strangers in Hyde Park."

A butler handed him a Union Jack umbrella and a script that read: "I'm dreadfully sorry, madam."

Ellie stared. "Wait, that was his sentence?"

Then a woman in pajamas was pushed onto the next float.

"CASE #3850! Sandra Whitmore—guilty of sneezing during the national anthem. Sentence: lifetime voucher for Greggs."

Ellie shot me a look. "Same crime, two completely different outcomes."

I responded, "yep. We're in random-justice territory."

The Reminder appeared beside us, wearing a tweed waistcoat and sipping PG Tips from a thermos labelled "Trust Me, I'm Legal."

"Welcome to the justice system of the future," he said. "Where laws are 'guidelines,' wigs are currency, and fairness has been replaced with tea-based bribery."

On the next float, a judge in a powdered wig and sequined robe banged a gavel shaped like a crumpet.

"CASE #3851! Oliver Twistleton—guilty of mismatched socks. Sentence: six months of interpretive Morris dancing on the Tube."

A man in bells and knee-high socks was already being shoved toward a Piccadilly line platform.

Ellie stood slowly. "This is either performance art... or the Ministry of Silly Walks got way too much power."

I watched a ten-year-old get sentenced to "forty seconds of royal bowing" for humming too loudly in a lift.

"This is ridiculous," I declared. "What even *is* this?"

Ellie crossed her arms. "Okay, this ends now."

She pointed at the judge on the jelly-bean float.

"No more pastry punishments. No more 'tea crimes.' We're fixing the system properly, with real laws."

The Reminder raised his cup in salute. "Good, because this one runs on biscuits and barely-contained chaos."

The shimmer swirled around us, smelling faintly of scones.

Time to put the real courtroom robes back on.

THIRTY-TWO

– 2025 –

JUSTICE WITH TEA
AND BISCUITS

SDG 16: Peace, Justice, and Strong Institutions

T his time, I landed in a chair.

An actual chair.

Not made of wood chips or recycled plastic, but a proper padded one you'd find in a community centre.

Ellie was beside me on a beanbag, sipping what looked like ribena (fruit drink) from a reusable bottle and blinking at our surroundings.

"Leyth," she said slowly, "did we just land in a town hall *tea and transparency* session?"

I looked around. We were inside a church hall in South London—string lights overhead, tables stacked with biscuits and complaint forms, and a poster that read:

"WELCOME TO THE BIG BOROUGH SIT-DOWN: Let's Fix Our Institutions Over a Cuppa."

The Reminder walked up wearing a knitted jumper with the Scales of Justice stitched across the front and holding a thermos labelled "Proper Brew."

"Told you," he said, unscrewing the lid. "Some of the best ideas begin with a cup of tea."

So we sat down at the borough meetings and collaborated with law students and professors, granny-led community groups, and that one retired English teacher who corrected everyone's grammar. Together, we rewrote the laws into clear, simple language that applied *consistently*, no matter who you were. Clarity brought confidence. Consistency brought trust.

Next, we launched mock trials in community centres where anyone could volunteer to play judge, jury, or snack table monitor. Ellie, from the bench: "Today's case is 'Who keeps leaving bikes in the stairwell?'"

The defendant (aka Mr. Jacobs from Flat 3B): "I plead innocent, Your Honour. My bike must have a mind of its own!"

The crowd? *Cackling.*

We set up digital reporting booths across the borough at libraries, post offices, and even chip shops.

Tap in your concern, get a sticker:

"I Stood Up For Justice and All I Got Was This Badge...and Some Real Change!"

People wore them like medals.

Even one old man stuck his on his dog's collar. The dog looked proud.

Eventually, instead of intimidating council meetings, we hosted informal drop-ins at local cafés and pubs. No speeches necessary, just officials and citizens around tables with scones and ideas.

That evening, the whole borough gathered in the park for a

"Justice Jubilee."

There were fairy lights, string quartets, and tables stacked with sandwiches arranged so precisely they could've been framed.

Kids drew cartoons about jury duty in chalk. Local MPs danced badly. A magistrate wore a glittery crown made of policy drafts.

The Reminder toasted us with elderflower cordial.

"This," he said, "is how you build trust; not by shouting louder, but by showing up, listening, and offering biscuits."

Ellie giggled. "Peace and justice with a side of biscuits."

I looked around, watching neighbours shake hands with councillors and teenagers teach adults how to use the feedback app.

The shimmer appeared near the bandstand.

Ellie bumped my arm. "SDG 16: Peace, justice, and strong institutions?"

I nodded. "Served with tea and slightly burnt jam tarts."

And together, we stepped into the light, full of hope and probably about five too many Jaffa Cakes.

THIRTY-THREE

−2220−

ONE COUNTRY, ONE BEACON

SDG 17: Partnerships for the Goals

I woke up in my bed.

Like, *my* bed. Not a radioactive swamp mattress. Not a crumbling rooftop. Not even a halfway-decent tree branch.

An actual bed with a pillow and a blanket. And sunshine slipping through my curtains like nothing had ever gone wrong with the world.

I blinked at the ceiling, halfway convinced this was some kind of time-travel-induced hallucination. Then my phone buzzed.

Ellie.

I picked up.

"Please tell me this is real," she said, not even bothering with hello.

"I was about to ask you the same thing."

"I just woke up in my bed."

"Same."

There was a pause. Then she said, "bike ride?"

"Be there in ten."

We met at the usual spot and pedaled through the quiet, sun-warmed streets. No smoke or sirens or even mutant squirrels throwing things at us from trees. Just birds chirping and the distant hum of solar buses.

We rode through Amman's restored neighborhoods, the Citadel rising in the distance. Flower boxes spilled over balconies. Gardens bloomed on rooftops. It was peaceful. Bright. *Right*.

"Okay," Ellie said, slowing beside me. "This is new."

I smiled. "This is *earned*."

We were in Amman, Jordan.

The streets were clean, lined with trees and flowers.

Public fountains ran with clear water, and kids laughed as they splashed each other.

Solar-powered buses glided by, as silent as cats.

The Citadel rose in the distance, but instead of ruins, it was fully restored and somehow blended seamlessly with the futuristic glass buildings around it.

And the rooftops?

Covered in gardens, actual, leafy, green gardens.

I half expected a Disney princess to pop out and start singing.

Ellie spun in a circle.

"This can't be real," she said.

I smiled. "It's real."

This wasn't just about one nation succeeding. It was about a blueprint for the entire world.

Jordan Did It

We wandered through the streets.

Vendors at the Souk sold solar-powered lanterns and local crafts.

Students crowded cafés, studying AI programming and agricultural science in the same breath.

Farmers' markets overflowed with produce grown in vertical gardens and desert-friendly farms.

Everywhere we went, people smiled. They were healthy, hopeful, and thriving.

Ellie stared at a street sign powered by wind energy.

"How did they do it?"

A voice answered behind us.

"They worked together."

The Reminder stood there, dressed like a diplomat, sharp suit and all, with a pin of the Jordanian flag on her lapel.

"They shared resources, supported their communities, prioritized sustainability over short-term gains."

Ellie looked around, wide-eyed.

"So... they won?"

The Reminder's smile was small.

"For now."

The Lonely Success

We sat in a rooftop café that evening, watching the sun set over Amman's glowing skyline.

The place looked like a dream with clean energy and water. There were thriving schools full of kids.

Hospitals were packed with technology, not patients.

Jordan was... a miracle.

"Why does it feel... temporary?" I asked.

The Reminder took a slow sip of mint tea.

"Because one country can't do it alone," she said.

She pointed out toward the horizon.

"This future isn't sustainable unless all nations work together.

Otherwise, Jordan will become a bright light surrounded by darkness."

No One Wins Alone

Ellie tapped her fingers on the table.

"So we have to convince everyone to work together?"

"Partnerships," I blurted out.

"That's the key," the Reminder agreed.

"Jordan is the example, but it can't be the exception."

Ellie was ready.

"Okay," she said. "Time to go global."

I grinned.

"World tour?"

"World tour."

She pulled out her tablet and started making a list.

"First stop?" she asked.

I looked out over the city, lights twinkling like stars.

"Everywhere."

The shimmer surrounded us.

This time, I wasn't afraid of where we'd land.

Because we weren't doing this for one country.

We were doing this for everyone.

THIRTY-FOUR

$-2025-$

THE FINAL MISSION

SDG 17: Partnerships for the Goals

T he next thing I knew, I was in a chair.

But not just any chair.

A fully reclining, buttery-soft, gold-stitched leather seat with a built-in massage function, chilled mango juice in the cupholder, and a touchscreen that said:

"Welcome aboard the Unity One. Destination: Everywhere."

Ellie gasped beside me, already halfway into a tray of complimentary snacks.

"Leyth," she whispered, eyes wide, "I think we just time-traveled into a luxury jet."

She looked down at her fully reclined seat. "With climate-controlled footrests."

I looked out the window.

Below us, Earth curved gently, blue and green and alive. Cities glittered like circuits on a motherboard. Rivers shimmered like veins.

Across from us, The Reminder sat in first class, legs crossed, sipping an iced hibiscus drink and wearing aviators like he'd been upgraded years ago.

"Finally," he said, "a landing that respects your contributions."

A flight attendant passed, handing us gourmet hummus and warm towels.

Ellie raised an eyebrow. "So... this is the finale?"

The Reminder swirled his drink. "This is the beginning of what happens when partnerships *actually work*. Welcome to the global collaboration tour."

Our job was simple.

Ha.

Convince countries around the world to work together, to share resources, tech, and knowledge, and to partner up, instead of trying to go solo.

No pressure.

Jordan had done it.

And they'd done it beautifully, but no one can do it alone.

Global Round-Up:
Because One Country Isn't Enough

We didn't stop.

We zipped from continent to continent like our jet ran on pure teamwork (and maybe a little solar fuel).

In Rwanda, we linked Jordan's mobile solar classrooms with local coding hubs: kids in Kigali were learning to build websites and solar panels in the same week.

In Vietnam, Hanoi's balcony farmers taught Amman how to green their rooftops, while Jordan shared their compost-to-energy tech in return.

In South Africa, we helped Cape Town and Amman co-design an anti-"Day Zero" water playbook, complete with shower timers, desalination hacks, and weirdly catchy conservation jingles.

In the U.K., we launched a cross-country youth innovation program: students solving real-world sustainability problems together, across time zones.

In the U.S., Jordan co-founded an AI sustainability think tank to tackle climate and inequality.

And in Morocco, desert towns from both nations started sharing solar microgrid tech like it was the new Wi-Fi password.

The world was learning from each other.

Finally.

The partnerships kept growing.

And every time they did, I felt the world get a little less heavy.

The shimmer of golden light surrounded us one last time.

I gasped as I felt the pull, but this time, it felt different.

This wasn't just a jump through time.

It was a jump back to the beginning.

THIRTY-FIVE

-2025-

WE WIN TOGETHER

The sound of squeaking sneakers and a bouncing basketball jolted me awake.

My heart pounded like I'd just run a marathon.

I opened my eyes.

No crumbling cities. No starving families. No mutant creatures.

Just... the gym.

The scoreboard buzzed, signaling the end of halftime. The crowd buzzed, their voices blending into one steady hum.

I was sitting on the bench, my jersey clinging to my sweaty skin.

Ellie stretched beside me, totally unaware that we had just rewritten history.

I stared at my hands, half-expecting them to shimmer or disappear or turn into robot claws (hey, it could happen).

But nope.

All good.

Except...had it all been real or just some insane dream?

I glanced around the gym, breathing in the smell of popcorn

and polished wood floors.

Normal.

Totally normal.

And yet—

The Note

There it was.

A folded note on the bench next to me.

I hadn't seen it there before.

Had it *always* been there?

Was I losing my mind?

(Answer: Probably.)

I picked it up slowly.

The handwriting was neat.

"Continue your teamwork, on and off the basketball court.

Because no one wins alone."

I looked at my teammates—Ellie, Ethan, the whole squad—waiting for me to rejoin them.

The team, the people I relied on.

I stood, tucking the note into my jersey. As I jogged toward the court, I glanced up at the bleachers.

And there she was.

The Reminder, half in shadow, sipping from a thermos.

She caught my eye... and winked.

I grinned.

"Alright, team!" I called. "Let's move the ball. We win this—together."

As I took my position, the crowd noise faded into the background.

Because this wasn't just about a game, it was about our future.

And this time?

We knew what we had to do...together.

Appendix: Learn More About the UN Sustainable Development Goals (SDGs)

1   General Information on SDGs

For a full overview of all 17 SDGs, visit these official UN pages:

- UN SDG Homepage – Overview of all goals, targets, and indicators
  https://sdgs.un.org/goals

- UN SDG Progress Report – The latest data on global SDG progress
  https://unstats.un.org/sdgs/report/

- UN SDG Action Campaign – Learn how to support SDGs through activism
  https://www.unsdgadvocates.org/

- UN SDG Media Zone – Articles, videos, and reports about SDGs
  https://www.un.org/sustainabledevelopment/sdg-media-zone/

2   SDGs in Action: How to Get Involved

Want to help make a difference? Here's where to start:

- ActNow Campaign (United Nations) – Simple actions to support SDGs in daily life
  https://www.un.org/en/actnow/

- The Lazy Person's Guide to Saving the World (UN Guide) – Easy ways to contribute to SDGs
  https://www.un.org/sustainabledevelopment/takeaction/

- Good Life Goals – How individuals can integrate SDGs into their lives
  https://sdghub.com/goodlifegoals/

3   SDG Educational & Research Resources

For those interested in learning more about SDGs, these sites provide data, reports, and learning materials:

- Global Goals by UNDP – Information about how countries implement SDGs
  https://www.globalgoals.org/

- SDG Tracker – Country-by-country data on SDG progress
  https://sdg-tracker.org/

- World Bank: SDGs & Global Development – Economic insights on SDGs
  https://datatopics.worldbank.org/sdgs/

- UNESCO & Education for SDGs – The role of education in achieving SDGs
  https://en.unesco.org/themes/education-sustainable-development

4   SDGs for Schools, Kids & Youth

Want to introduce SDGs to students, young activists, or educators? These resources are made for kids and young changemakers:

- UNICEF's SDGs for Children & Youth – How young people can engage with SDGs
  https://www.unicef.org/sdgs

- World's Largest Lesson – Free lessons, resources, and activities for students
  https://worldslargestlesson.globalgoals.org/

- Earth School (TED-Ed & UNEP) – Interactive environmental education for students
  https://ed.ted.com/earth-school

5   SDGs for Businesses & Innovation

For entrepreneurs, business leaders, and investors looking to align their work with SDGs:

- UN Global Compact – How businesses can integrate SDGs into their strategy
  https://www.unglobalcompact.org/

- SDG Impact (For Entrepreneurs & Investors) – Frameworks for responsible business
  https://sdgimpact.undp.org/

- World Economic Forum: SDGs & Global Impact – How SDGs shape the future of business
  https://www.weforum.org/agenda/archive/sustainable-development-goals

6   UN Reports & Global Policies on SDGs

For policy makers, researchers, and journalists, these are key sources:

- High-Level Political Forum on Sustainable Development – Official UN meetings & decisions on SDGs
  https://hlpf.un.org/

- Sustainable Development Knowledge Platform – UN policies, reports, and best practices
  https://sustainabledevelopment.un.org/

A special thanks to my grandfather,
Sherif Fawaz Sharaf El-Hashemite,
whose unwavering belief in me gives me the
confidence to pursue my dreams and make a
difference. Your legacy of guidance and
love will forever be woven into these pages.